Investigating Social Issues

ECONOMICS TODAY
Edited by Andrew Leake

The *Economics Today* series surveys contemporary headline topics in applied economics. Each book in the series is written by an expert in the field in a style that is fluently readable. It serves the student of introductory economic principles while also making the subject accessible to a more general reader. The series embraces the problem-solving skills of the new generation of students and stresses the importance of real-world issues and the significance of economic ideas.

Published

Andrew Leake: **The Economic Question**
Jean-Louis Barsoux and Peter Lawrence: **The Challenge of British Management**
S. F. Goodman: **The European Community**
Jenny Wales: **Investigating Social Issues**

Forthcoming
Frank Burchill: **Labour Relations**

INVESTIGATING SOCIAL ISSUES

Jenny Wales

palgrave
macmillan

First published 1990

Published by
MACMILLAN EDUCATION LTD
Houndmills, Basingstoke, Hampshire RG21 2XS
and London
Companies and representatives
throughout the world

This book is printed on paper suitable for recycling and made from fully managed and sustained forest sources. Logging, pulping and manufacturing processes are expected to conform to the environmental regulations of the country of origin.

British Library Cataloguing in Publication Data
Wales, Jenny
Investigating social issues. — (Economics today).
1. Economics, related to sociology
I. Title II. Series
330
ISBN 978-0-333-51831-1 (hardback)
ISBN 0–333–51832–2 (paperback)

Contents

List of Tables and Figures

Tables

Figures

1 What Do We Have Government For?

'Uproar Greets Great Tax Reforms'

'Lots of Lovely Lolly'

'The Ladies' Man'

'Chancellor Brings Cheer to the Wealthy'

'The Tax Terminator'

'Chancellor's Tax Triumph'

The headlines above all appeared on the morning after a recent Budget. The Chancellor's decisions had sparked very different responses from the newspapers, both in terms of attitude and focus of attention. Why can opinion vary as much as this?

Some people think that the market should be the controlling influence in the economy, others feel that the government should intervene more in events. This results from the value judgements that they make, in other words, they have different lists of priorities. In the case of the Budget, one group of people felt that the money would be used more efficiently in the hands of taxpayers while others thought that the government should have used it to help poorer members of the population.

Political parties base their decisions on the value judgements which underlie their philosophy. Every year, in the Budget they have two sets of decisions to make. First of all, they must decide how much they want to raise and how to raise it, and secondly, how to spend it. In order to do this they have to decide what they regard as important.

All governments are faced with the problem of limited resources or scarcity. Even one which believes its major role is to redistribute income and therefore has high levels of taxation cannot raise enough money to do everything it thinks necessary. It has to make choices and it bases these on a ranking of objectives.

What Are the Choices for Government Expenditure?

Health	Unemployment
Defence	Overseas aid
Education	Environment
Industry	Transport
Arts	Housing
Pensions	Science
Energy	Benefits

These are some of the possible ways a government might choose to spend its money. The list is by no means exhaustive and all governments will have to devote some of their spending to each of them. Just how much will depend on relative positions in the order of priorities. It is this ranking that varies between the main political parties. In Britain, we make the fundamental choice about which list of priorities we want at election time and then leave the party that wins to make detailed decisions on how to spend the money.

How Much Should the Government Spend?

Although many people perceive an enormous gap between the

FIGURE 1.1
Comparative Government Expenditure as a Proportion of GDP
(excluding transfers such as pensions or benefits)

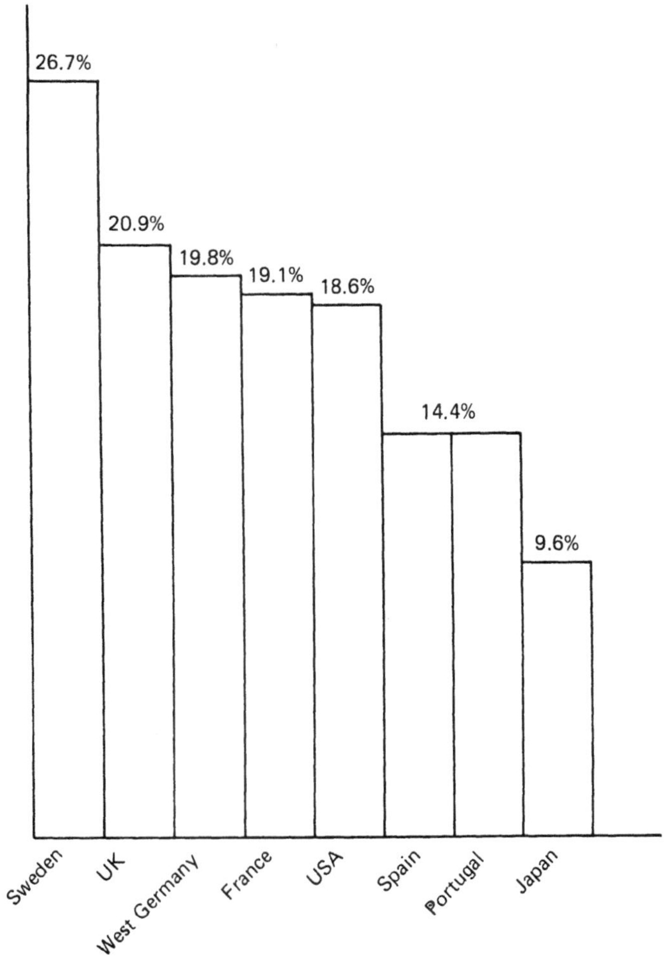

SOURCE: *OECD Economic Survey 1989.*

decisions taken by our political parties, on the spectrum of possibilities they are not really very far apart. A comparison between the decisions taken in the USSR and America would show much greater extremes because of the different levels of government interference in those economies.

Despite changes that are taking place in the USSR, the economy is still highly centralised whereas in America the market is left to rule in most sectors. In Britain, we have a mixed economy which falls somewhere between the two, depending on the nature of the current government.

Throughout the world different countries choose to make their spending decisions in different ways. Figure 1.1 shows the degree of variation in government expenditure between some of the countries which belong to the Organisation for Economic Cooperation and Development (OECD). Despite the fact that the USA is a country that we think of as market dominated, its government spending is relatively high. Let's compare the two extremes within the OECD, Sweden and Japan. In spite of the fact that they are both democratic countries, the Swedish government spends three times as much as the Japanese, as a percentage of GDP. The Swedes believe that the state should provide a high standard of education, health care and welfare benefits for everyone, so taxation and government spending are both high. The Japanese, however, believe that many of these services should be left to the market. None of the countries on the graph is 'right' or 'wrong'. The decisions will depend on the value judgements made by the electorate and how they are put into practice by the government.

What Has Happened in the UK?

Figure 1.2 shows that much more significant factors than the nature of the government in power influence the level of spending. The trend throughout this century has been upwards with two major leaps during the wars. These both had a ratchet effect as post-war spending did not fall back to pre-war levels. The irregularities on the graph reflect the policies of different governments. This can be seen clearly in the mid-1970s when spending rose and the 1980s when spending fell as a proportion of Gross Domestic Product. When looked at in terms of actual goods and services that government spending can buy, the picture looks rather different.

FIGURE 1.2
General Government Expenditure, 1890–1986 (percentage of GDP)

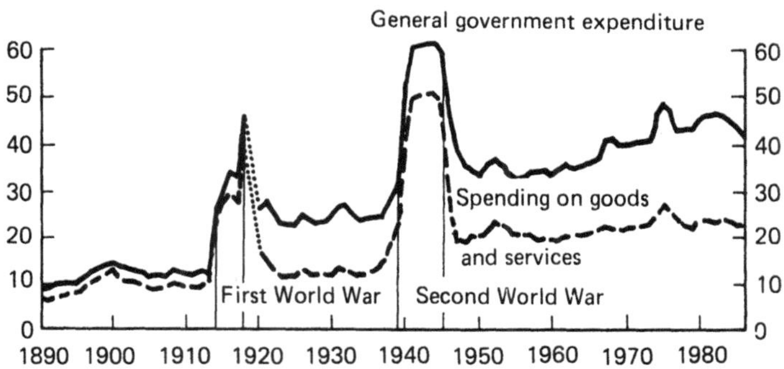

Figures not available for 1919.
SOURCE: *Economic Progress Report* (HM Treasury), February 1988.

TABLE 1.1
Spending Under Labour and Conservative Governments (At 1980 prices in £ million)

	Labour		*Conservative*	
Central Government	*1978*	*1979*	*1980*	*1981*
Military defence	10 404	10 587	11 328	11 317
National Health Service	10 719	11 112	11 249	11 522
Other	7 384	7 398	7 242	7 219
Total	28 579	29 097	29 851	30 085
Local Authorities				
Education	8 880	9 050	9 005	8 788
Other	9 666	9 960	9 954	9 965
Total	18 546	19 010	18 959	18 753

SOURCE: *United Kingdom National Accounts 1984* (HMSO).

FIGURE 1.3
General Government Expenditure in Real Terms (£ billion)

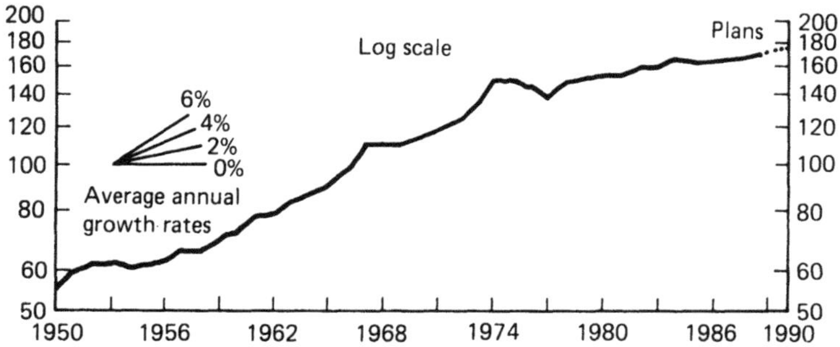

* Real terms figures are the cash figures adjusted to 1986–7 price levels by excluding the effect of general inflation as measured by the GDP deflator.
† The different slopes of the lines represent different rates of annual growth. The steeper the gradient, the greater the growth rate. By comparing the slopes with particular sections of the graph the reader can determine the appropriate rate of annual growth over that period.
Note Figures for the period 1950 to 1960 are in calendar years. 1961–2 to 1990–1 are in financial years. Figures not available for 1919.

Figure 1.3 shows that although government spending may fall as a percentage of GDP it rarely falls in real terms. Why is this? We must presume that government spending is a result of government's decisions, and so reflects a rising demand for public goods and services. But which goods and services matter most and where does this demand originate? This, of course, is partly political.

Changes in government seem to bring significant changes in the pattern of spending, as shown in Table 1.1 on the previous page. The Labour government was replaced by the Conservatives in 1979. The rate of growth of spending accelerated in defence but slowed down in the health service. Local authority spending on education actually fell in real terms.

Total central government consumption rose more rapidly than before in the first full year of the new government. It slowed down thereafter. This demonstrates the priorities of different political parties. But the overall level of real spending has risen under all governments, suggesting a deeper economic argument.

What Is the Government Trying To Do?

Whatever a government's value judgements, there are two fundamental principles which must be balanced when making spending decisions: equity and efficiency (Figure 1.4).

Equity is a question of how fairly resources are distributed between people. Chapter 8 on Income Distribution shows how equity and equality are not the same thing. At what point can any allocation be said to be just? We are again in the realms of value judgements so decisions about equity are political rather than economic. They are also fundamentally involved in policy-making. Economists think they are on safer ground when investigating

FIGURE 1.4
Equity and Efficiency: A Trade-off?

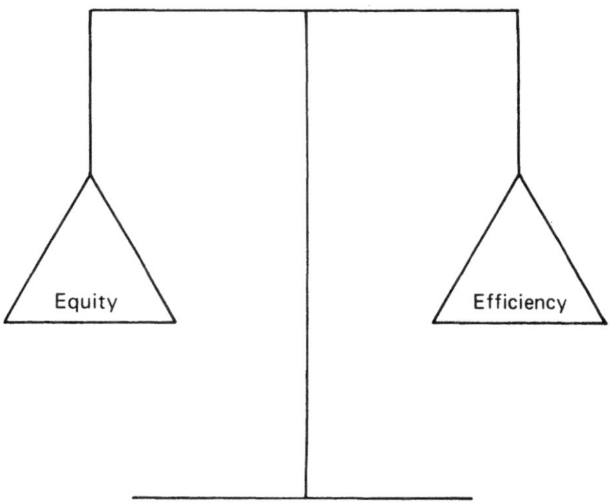

efficiency, but even here they are not really making value-free judgements. Chapters 3 and 4 on Education and Health both highlight these problems. Often decisions about efficiency assume current income levels as their starting point. In doing so they are accepting current value judgements.

We can, however, attempt to measure *cost efficiency*. It is defined as the point where there is the maximum difference between benefits to consumers and costs of production. The idea can be applied to any form of production, from a traffic cone for the M25 to the Channel Tunnel. Figure 1.5 shows how we apply this idea to total costs and benefits. Chapter 9 on Transport demonstrates the use of costs and benefits in this way.

The total social benefit curve shows that people receive less benefit the more they consume, because they receive most satisfaction from the first item of any product and less from subsequent ones. The benefit from too many pints of beer rapidly becomes negative.

FIGURE 1.5
Total Social Costs and Benefits

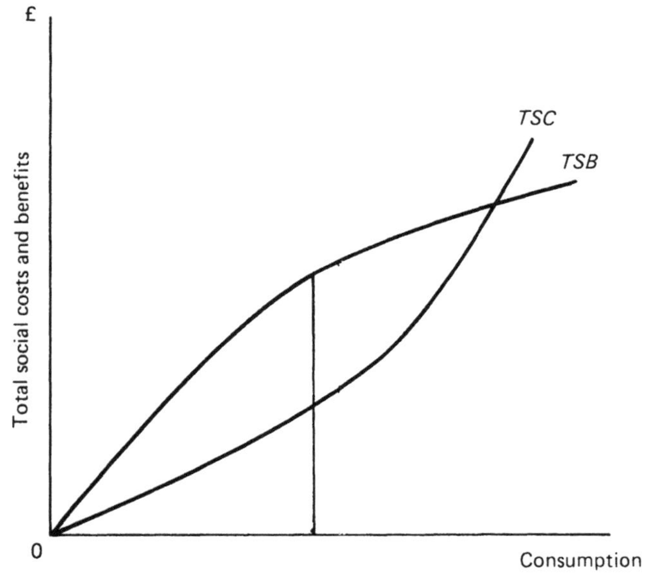

The total social cost curve shows that as more is produced costs rise. The costs to the firm may rise because it will be difficult to produce efficiently as it moves beyond the best output level for their factory. The costs to society may rise if the methods of production involve polluting the environment, causing congestion and so on. The most efficient point to produce is where the two curves are furthest apart as this provides the greatest benefit for the least cost. The same idea can be expressed in another way in terms of the additional cost and additional benefit, or marginal cost and benefit offered by one extra unit.

Figure 1.6 shows that there is no point in producing goods once the marginal social costs have risen above marginal social benefit. If marginal benefit exceeds marginal cost production should be increased. Total benefit arises ahead of total costs and society is gaining. If marginal cost exceeds marginal benefit, production should be cut, since total cost is catching up with total benefit. The

FIGURE 1.6
Marginal Social Costs and Benefits

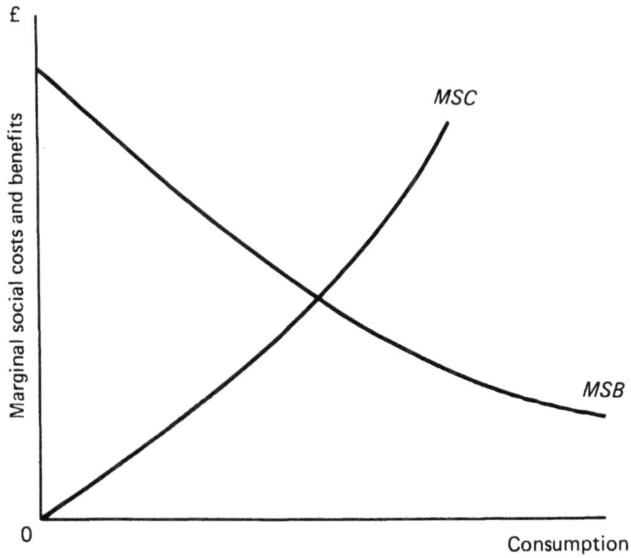

total gap is greatest and efficiency is realised where marginal social benefit exactly equals marginal social cost.

This analysis can be used to find the efficient level of production for anything. It applies equally well to private goods, produced by profit-making individuals and public goods, produced collectively by the state. We can use it to investigate social issues such as health care, education or the environment.

We have, so far, assumed that equity and efficiency are the only aims of a government. In fact they have to compete with other objectives such as freedom and civil liberties. For example, producing goods efficiently is not necessarily compatible with freedom of movement. If labour could be directed to areas of the country where production costs were low, total efficiency would increase, but in a democratic country such measures would prove unacceptable except in crises such as wartime.

Efficiency stresses the motive of self-interest, but recent trends in society have encouraged the role of giving. Disasters throughout the world have stimulated a much more generous response than in the past. Bandaid, Live-aid, Sportaid and Comic Relief are just a few of the techniques which have been devised to persuade people to part with their money to help the less fortunate. Charity and sponsorship can replace several of the functions of government.

Why Should the Government Interfere with Market Forces?

There are some things which every government feels the need to provide. The level of provision may give scope for argument, but no party that wants to win the next election will abolish state education or the National Health Service. Why does everyone agree that there are some areas that cannot be ignored? What would happen if all education or health care had to be paid for privately? *Some people would go without.* But poor people go without all sorts of things, of course. What makes these services different is their value, through consumption, to others in the population.

Public goods tend not to be provided by the market because it is impossible to persuade individuals to pay for them. People will buy private goods like compact disc players or a car because they can take them home and use them, but public goods cannot be kept at home, they cannot be used up and everyone else will benefit from your consumption – so why should you pay for them? The common examples are national defence and street lights. It would be very hard to run an army on the basis of everyone paying for their own soldier and many people would simply opt out, but still benefit from the protection provided by others. Such people are known as 'free-riders'. These goods have some other characteristics. They are *non-diminishable*, in other words, they can't be used up. This means that it is difficult to calculate an individual's contribution to the costs. Likewise, they are *indivisible*. One soldier or the tenth of a street light are not much use.

Merit goods are things which are socially desirable. They can be provided by the market and in some countries this is their only source. However, in most of the developed world, governments provide these things to a greater or lesser extent. The amount of provision is going to depend on the political complexion of the government of each country. Education is the most universal merit good. Health care is a close second but governments' contributions vary considerably even in Western Europe. Enabling everyone to benefit from education and health care has economic consequences that are for the general good. If the population is fit and well educated they will be more productive and the general standard of living will rise.

The government also has to spend money on controlling demerit goods such as firearms and drugs which may be misused because their effects are irreversible. It is difficult to isolate goods which fall into this category except by banning or controlling them. In other cases, such as alcohol and tobacco, heavy taxes are levied which limit demand and increase government revenue. The success of this policy will depend on the nature of people's demand for the product. This is shown in Figure 1.7.

Demand and supply are essential tools for explaining free market behaviour: demand simply reflects how much people want to buy at a particular price; supply shows how much firms want to sell at a particular price. Usually demand rises as the price falls and vice versa because people have the income to afford more at lower prices and choose more in preference to other alternatives. Supply rises as the price rises because firms want to make more profit over their costs. Together, demand and supply set market price.

Elasticity shows how much demand and supply changes when price changes. Demand is inelastic when we go on buying much the same amount, even when the price goes up. It is inelastic when we substantially reduce our purchases of cars or foreign holidays, for example, when the price goes up.

If demand is elastic it is much easier to persuade people not to buy, because if the price goes up they will reduce consumption more than proportionately. However, if demand is inelastic it is more difficult because raising the price will have a less than proportionate effect on how much is bought. These two situations are shown by Figures 1.7 and 1.8.

FIGURE 1.7
If Demand Is Elastic a Tax Will Reduce Consumption

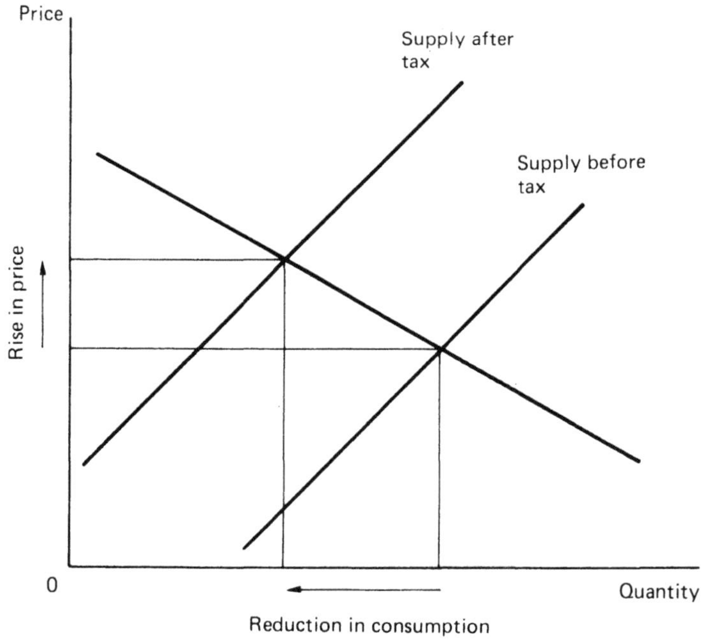

FIGURE 1.8
If Demand Is Inelastic a Tax Will Have Little Effect on Consumption

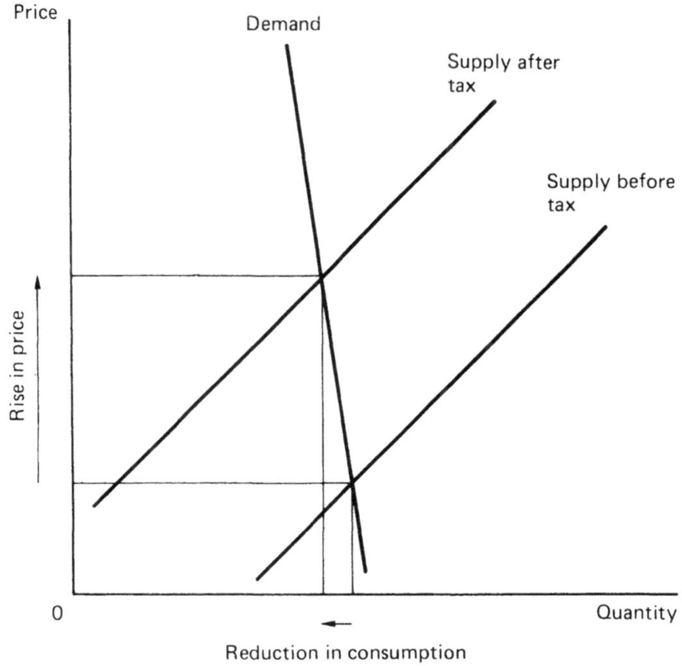

Does the Market Always Give the *Best* Allocation of Resources?

When the market is the dominant feature of an economy, profit will generally determine what is available to buy. Producers of goods and services will want to incur the lowest possible costs, so achieving cost efficiency within the firm. They also want to sell their output at the highest possible price and to set output so as to maximise profit. In order to achieve the lowest possible costs, manufacturers may ignore the effect that they are having on the world around them. The chemical works will pump its effluent into the sea or the fossil fuel power station will let noxious gases escape into the air. It's much cheaper to do this than to clean up the waste products before disposing of them. So who does pay the cost of these firms' economies?

There are two answers to this question. If nothing is done, the environment pays the penalty. The River Thames is only just recovering from years of neglect. It was once a spawning ground for salmon but it became so badly polluted that they all disappeared. The cost of cleaning it up fell on society as a whole. The Thames Water Authority polices the river and ensures that the anti-pollution laws are kept. Salmon are, at last, beginning to reappear.

These side-effects of production are known as *externalities* and they arise in all areas of the economy. Driving your car to work and back causes congestion and adds to pollution and therefore has external effects on other people. The costs that are incurred by the individual or the firm are known as *private costs*. In the examples above they are going to be less than those borne by the economy as a whole. These are called *social costs*. The following equation shows the relationship between them.

$$\text{Private Costs} + \text{Externalities} = \text{Social Costs}$$

If firms are not paying the full cost of producing their goods, because someone else is cleaning up the mess they make, the price that people pay for them is lower than it should be. If the price is low, more will be demanded and more resources will be devoted to their production. Figure 1.9 shows the effect on output and price of ignoring some of the costs of production.

Firms which do pay to clean up their effluent will obviously be at a disadvantage. Their costs and therefore their prices will be much higher, so they will be able to sell fewer goods. As demand will be lower, less resources will be allocated to the production of these items. The market is therefore failing to ensure that firms work in the interests of society as a whole because more profit can be made by ignoring the environment.

If the allocation of resources is to be efficient the marginal cost must be equal to price in all industries. With no externalities this is enough to ensure that $MSB = MSC$ as before. Such an ideal situation is known as *allocative efficiency*. But the natural state of affairs is for externalities to occur and for other complications to limit productive efficiency. If we are to attempt to move towards a situation where resources are used in the best way, the government

FIGURE 1.9
The Effect on Demand of Ignoring the Costs of Pollution

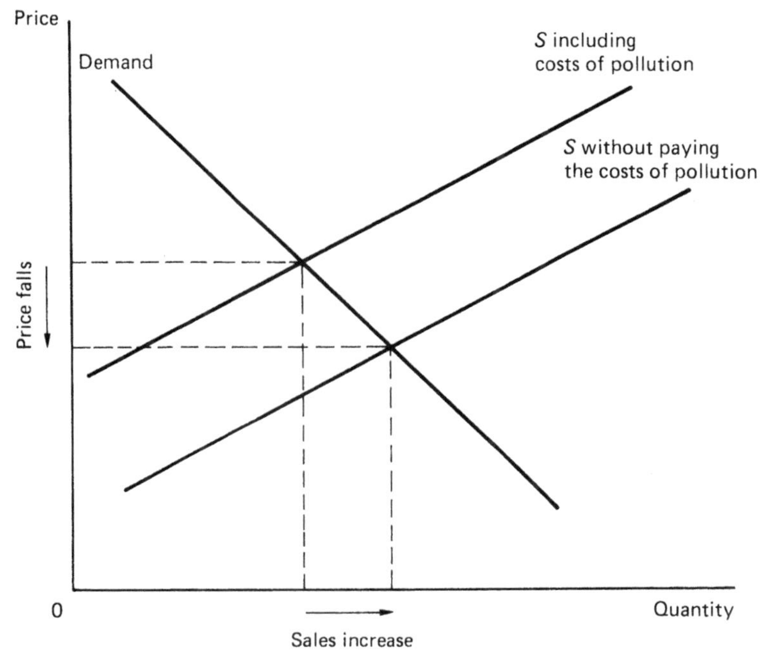

will have to intervene. The degree of intervention will depend on the value judgements made by each government. Chapter 5, Conservation and the Environment, takes this debate further.

How Can the Government Intervene?

In order to achieve something approaching allocative efficiency, a government has to interfere with the market mechanism. The problem can be dealt with either by trying to make the market more perfect or by reducing the effects of the externalities caused by its failure.

Regional policy is an attempt to overcome market failure. In

Chapters 6, The Inner Cities, and 7, Regional Policy, the differing attitudes to overcoming the inefficient allocation of resources and therefore helping the poorer parts of the country are examined.

A monopoly also demonstrates how markets fail. It has the power to make excess profits by raising prices or restricting output because it is the dominant firm in the market. This is the most extreme form of imperfect market and leads to misallocation of resources. The consumers lose because they are paying more for the goods they buy, or choosing to do without, and the monopolist gains as he is making excess profit. Society as a whole is losing because *MSB* is not equal to *MSC*. Governments make laws which prevent monopolies developing, either by stopping mergers if they give too much control to one firm, or by outlawing price and output agreements between firms.

Attempts to reduce the effects of market failure are usually made through the law, direct provision, taxes and subsidies. These methods are used in a variety of contexts as we will see in later chapters, but are briefly outlined here.

The return of salmon to the River Thames has been brought about through legislation. The government imposed stringent controls on the discharge of waste products into rivers and has given the water authorities powers to enforce these rules. This means that factories on the banks of rivers have to turn externalities into private costs and therefore reduce society's liability. Prices of their products will rise to cover all costs so less will be demanded and the allocation of resources will become more efficient. A legal solution has to be used when it is difficult to track down the perpetrators. No one will fill in a form admitting that they plan to pollute the river so a tax is impossible to impose. In later chapters we will see how legal measures are applied in a variety of situations.

Public and merit goods are not adequately provided by the market. In many cases, the use of legal controls or taxation would not improve the situation so the government simply has to replace the market system and supply these requirements itself. The chapters on health, education and housing all show how this happens. By doing this the government is reallocating resources and improving both equity and efficiency as a result.

Making things more expensive is a good way of persuading people not to indulge in certain activities or at least pay the true cost of their provision. The government uses this policy to reduce smoking and drinking (although raising revenue is a good reason too!). It is also a possible solution for the control of road congestion (Chapter 9) and pollution (Chapter 5) but is quite difficult to apply in these circumstances, as we shall see later on.

Subsidies work in the opposite way to taxation. By making some things cheaper, a higher percentage of the population will be able to buy so the allocation of resources will improve. Grants for students, for example, which are discussed in Chapter 3, are a subsidy which enables more people to benefit from higher education.

2 Housing

HOUSING SHORTAGE IS BLAMED FOR ACUTE MANPOWER CRISIS

Crawley personnel managers have found themselves in the 'crazy' situation of discussing the local labour shortage while elsewhere in Britain there is high unemployment. More than 100 managers from Gatwick firms and local industrial and commercial companies attended a special Institute of Personnel Management, Crawley Group, meeting to discuss the 'Mid Sussex Crisis' of manpower shortage.

They fear that with the expansion of Gatwick and other local companies, thousands of people will want to move into the area but be unable to because of an acute housing shortage. A human resources management consultant claimed that the problems faced by a teacher who moved down from Newcastle highlights the housing problem. Because houses are in short supply and the demand is so great the man, who has sold his north-east home after repaying several years mortgage, only had enough money to afford a deposit on an inferior house.

He added, 'I do not want to see the green fields where I live covered with houses, but I do not think we are going to have a lot of choice.'

Adapted from the *Crawley Observer*, 22 February 1986.

In Britain we are faced with a variety of housing problems. Crawley's difficulties reflect one end of the spectrum; that of having plenty of jobs available but no one to fill them because there is not enough housing. There is such great demand for houses in this area that prices have increased beyond the reach of people who live in those parts of the country which have high unemployment.

The other side of the picture can be seen on Merseyside, in South Wales or other regions which have suffered from the changing structure of the British economy. The income from selling a three-bedroomed semi-detached house in these areas will scarcely buy a flat in the South East. People are deterred from moving their families in order to find a job elsewhere. The downturn in house prices in the late 1980s has had little impact on the differential between the regions.

The chance of finding rented accommodation is just as remote. There are already 1.5 million families on council waiting lists so public housing does not provide the solution. Private landlords have been selling up for two reasons. Until recently, the laws which protect tenants by controlling rents had reduced their profit margins. Secondly, rising property prices meant that selling was more attractive than continuing to let.

The number of houses offered for sale may change greatly from time to time but the overall supply of accommodation to the community cannot. Although buildings may last for hundreds of years new ones take some time to build. Sites must be bought, prepared and passed for building permission. Materials and building firms must be employed and even then the structure may take a year or two to assemble and finish. There is always a time-lag in production which is demonstrated by the cobweb pattern of Figure 2.1. Excess demand may result in more houses being built, but developers tend to overestimate and start too many houses so excess supply results. As the pattern continues equilibrium is never reached.

The pattern of demand as well as supply has changed. Every small family unit now expects to have its own home. In the past, it has been very common to have three, if not four, generations living in the same house, but now children want to leave and set up on their own. As more old people live independently and more families break up, the demand for flats and other small homes has risen greatly since the war.

Essentially, however, housing demand is based on purchasing power. Rising real incomes, especially in the prosperous South East, are supported by more flexible and generous mortgage finance.

FIGURE 2.1
The Effect of the Time-lag in Building Houses

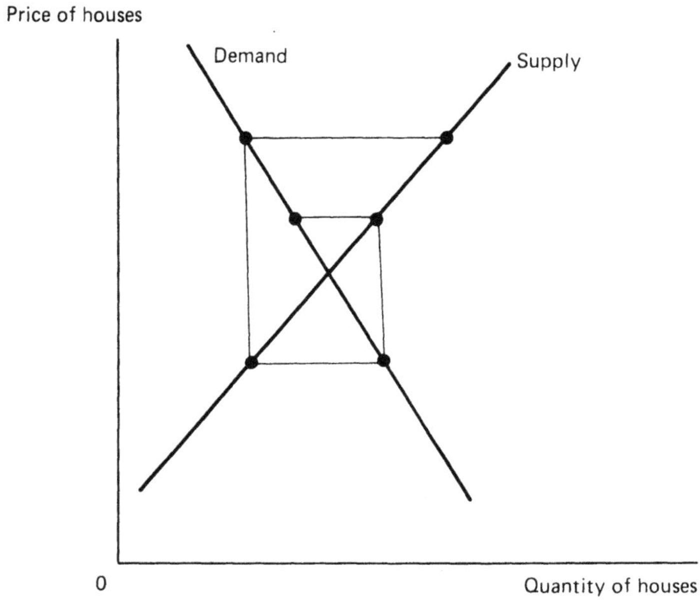

People choose to spend their extra money on housing, for immediate consumption benefit and as a long-term investment.

The 'north–south divide' has affected the market significantly and the difficulties faced by Crawley are a reflection of this. As new industries grow and develop in the South East, the demand for houses has far outstripped supply with the resulting increase in price. In the peripheral regions, where job losses have been high, demand has fallen as some people have been trying to sell in order to move away and others have had little money to buy within the area.

The Benefits of Housing to the Economy

Inadequate provision of housing creates extra costs, or externalities, for the whole economy. It limits growth and pushes up government spending both directly and indirectly.

Output in Crawley cannot increase if the labour supply is inadequate. If this pattern is repeated throughout the economy the effect on the Gross Domestic Product will be significant, as the country will be unable to reach its potential level of production because it cannot use its available resources efficiently.

The only way to attract labour may be to offer higher and higher wages in order to help meet housing costs, but this would represent a substantial increase in costs and therefore prices would have to rise. Sales of goods made in these high cost areas would be affected both at home and abroad and the country's trading situation would deteriorate.

MAKING A MEAL OF THE BED AND BREAKFAST TRAP

Tina, a soft spoken 18 year old, lives in a hotel with a stucco front in Bayswater with Derek, her 10-month-old son. Moisture stains the walls of their small room and the only chair is a three-legged affair, lacking a seat. The room is up five flights of stairs, with one tiny window looking out on a cement wall.

For this the grand-daddy of welfare states pays £32 a night or £11,680 a year – nearly what the average Londoner earns and well above the rent for a furnished studio apartment in many upmarket neighbourhoods here.

Tina is enmeshed in one of the world's most expensive – and ironic – housing programmes. Along with other major cities, London is struggling to cope with the army of homeless families.

'This is an insane use of resources,' says John R. Hill, a senior research fellow at the London School of Economics. Building a new house in London would cost about £50,000, he estimates. 'So within five years you're wasting on bed and breakfast a number that would have covered a whole new dwelling. This is clearly lunatic.

Adapted from the *Wall Street Journal*, Europe

Councils have a legal responsibility to house the homeless, but because of the limited supply of public housing they have had to resort to the use of bed and breakfast accommodation. The problem has been exacerbated by the disappearance of cheap flats as areas have been 'gentrified'. As property values have risen private landlords have sold up. Another factor which has made the situation worse is the government's policy of selling council houses. By the late 1980s, 61 000 properties had been sold in London, so the stock has been considerably reduced.

In London, 7300 homeless families live in these hotels, a number which has grown eightfold since 1981. The borough of Camden spent 9.6 per cent of its budget, equivalent to £15.5 million, on hotels for the homeless in the year ending in March 1988. London, as a whole, spent nearly £100 million in the same year, a figure which could clearly be allocated more efficiently to other uses. The only people who are benefiting from this 'lunatic' system are the hotel owners. Tourists are seasonal; the homeless are with us all the year round.

Social Costs

The main objective of government housing policy is to provide everyone with 'a decent home', which means that no one's home should fall beneath a minimum standard. This places housing as a 'necessity' so public demand would be totally inelastic at that minimum standard. The objectives in this area, therefore, tend to be expressed in terms of equity rather than efficiency.

The article about bed and breakfast accommodation says very clearly that we are not achieving our aims. Tina's room with peeling, damp walls cannot be described as 'a decent home' and certainly meets few requirements of equity. The value judgements behind the logic that permits this to continue ignores the externalities involved.

Society, in the end, bears the brunt of such poor provision because the bad side-effects or negative externalities which result from inadequate housing are expensive to deal with in both human and financial terms. Girls in Tina's situation often find it difficult to cope and the child goes into care and a hostel bed has to be found for the mother. Apart from the cost of accommodation for them both, the cost of a social worker's time must be taken into account. Families who live in poor quality housing tend to suffer because of it. Damp rooms lead to ill-health and recovery is difficult because cooking facilities may be inadequate and low incomes result in a lack of money to buy good food.

Maria has lived in a hotel in Earl's Court for nineteen months, since just before her son was born. The only time the boy has lived outside the hotel was in February, when he was hospitalised with a chipped leg bone caused by a vitamin D deficiency. Mother and son eat mostly carry out pizzas and baked potatoes because they don't have a kitchen.

Adapted from the *Wall Street Journal*

Maria's problems have created considerable costs for the economy. The state is paying for her hotel accommodation, help from social services and an increased health care bill because of their poor diet. As children grow older the problems of health and unstable housing mean that they miss out on education and this puts them into a continuing cycle of deprivation. It will not be easy to get a job with a poor school record and they may find themselves in the same position as Tina or Maria.

Would it be more efficient, in the long run, to provide adequate housing?

Even with help from the state we have not yet succeeded in providing 'a decent home' for the entire population. Housing is a *merit good* and thought to be socially desirable, so local authorities have an important role in ensuring a socially efficient provision. Central government in the 1980s aimed to make the market work more efficiently through increased home ownership, the revival of the private rented sector and developments which encourage private finance to take a role in housing.

Government Strategies to Encourage Home Ownership

The Conservative government regards home ownership as 'the principal foundation of the property owning democracy'. In the 1980s, 25 per cent more families became home owners and Britain reached the top of the league as 64 per cent of our dwellings became owner occupied (Table 2.1).

Several strategies have been used to encourage this growth. The most controversial has been the 'right to buy' which has enabled tenants in local authority housing to buy their properties at prices that take into account the rent that has been paid in the past. Over 1.1 million tenants have bought their homes since changes in the law made it possible. Even the Labour Party has included this policy in

TABLE 2.1
Owner-occupation in Europe

Country	*Owner-occupied dwellings as a % of total*
United Kingdom	64
Belgium	61
Italy	59
France	51
Netherlands	44
West Germany	37
Switzerland	30

SOURCE: 'Key Facts' (London: The Building Societies Association, 1989).

its election manifesto so it has obviously been very popular with those who have been able to buy. They have, however, stipulated that income from sales will go towards new housing.

Attempts have been made to reduce the cost of buying houses by removing the conveyancing monopoly held by solicitors, in the hope that competition would reduce fees. A major change in the housing market has come about because of the growing availability of mortgage funds. The market has widened as banks have taken a much more important role and building societies have become more competitive. In the 1970s, people had to wait in a queue until there was money available for them to borrow. Now the banks frequently mail their customers with offers of funds.

House ownership has continued to be subsidised through the tax system as income tax is not paid on interest on mortgages up to £30 000. There are anomalies in this system. It is thought by some people to be an anomaly as it is benefiting people who can already afford to buy a house but provides nothing for those who are generally less well off and have to rent. The second anomaly is that it helps those who are paying higher rate tax as they get relief on the top rate they pay, which may be up to 40 per cent.

As subsidies reduce the price of owning a house, demand will increase. Supply then rises as the market grows so more people are able to buy. Figure 2.2 reflects this effect and shows why the government is not keen to change the law at a time when they are trying to encourage home ownership.

In order to make more houses available for sale new building has been necessary. To facilitate this the government has given grants for clearing derelict sites and urban regeneration. Half the new homes built recently have been on such sites and therefore do not impinge on the rural environment. The other half have been on green field sites and battles are constantly being fought over intrusions into the green belt.

The measures have led to an increase in private building. In 1987, more houses were built than in any year since 1973. A total of 191 500 were started and 170 200 were completed.

FIGURE 2.2
The Effect of a Subsidy on Home Ownership

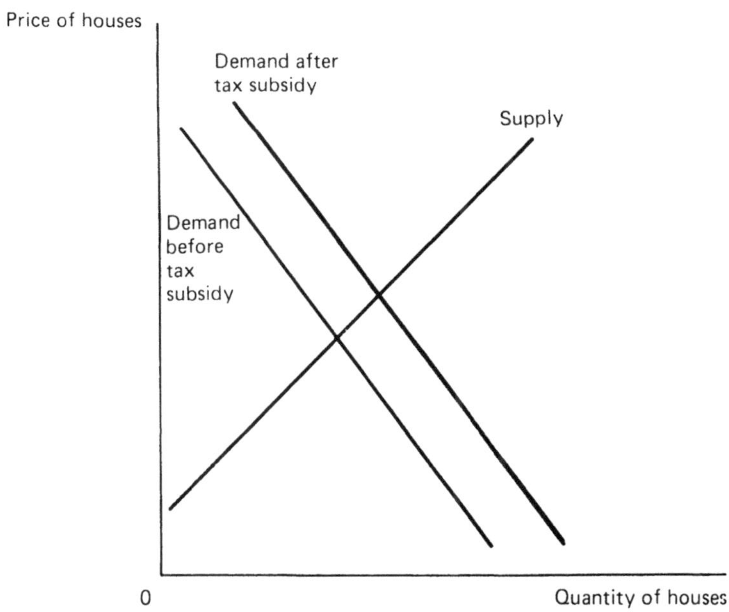

Despite the popularity of the 'Right To Buy' policy, drawbacks to the encouragement of home ownership became apparent. The diminishing public sector housing stock has not been replenished by new building, so there is less than before the policy was put into practice. The properties that are sold are usually the pleasant houses with gardens so the run-down tower blocks are left for the less fortunate. Laying stress on the private sector has therefore led to reduced public provision.

Many people have been persuaded that purchasing is a wise decision, only to be faced with problems that they cannot cope with. In the past they did not need to worry about maintenance as the upkeep of the house has been the duty of the local authority. The costs of external decoration or retiling a roof can come as a shock. Mortgage rate fluctuations must also be taken into account as they may make a large hole in a domestic budget. These events, together with unexpected unemployment, help to explain the increase in building societies' repossessions of properties (Table 2.2).

TABLE 2.2
Building Society Repossessions

Year	*Properties taken into possession by building societies*
1979	2,530
1980	3,020
1981	4,240
1982	5,950
1983	7,320
1984	10,870
1985	16,770
1986	20,930
1987	22,930
1988	16,150

SOURCE: *Building Society News* 1989

The figures reached a peak in the first half of 1987 and have started to fall since then, a dramatic decline occurring in 1988. The downward trend is probably related to economic growth, falling unemployment and building societies' changing attitudes to those in trouble with payments.

'Freedom of choice' is the main argument in favour of increasing home ownership. As state provision is lower, less is taken in taxation so individuals' assets increase and they have more opportunity to decide how to spend their money. The system works well provided that there is adequate back-up for those who for any reason are unable to look after themselves or their families.

Reviving the Private Rented Sector

In Britain, the private rented sector represents a very small proportion of the total housing stock, whereas in the rest of Europe the private landlord has a much more important role. In Germany, 43 per cent of homes are rented from private landlords and in France the figure is 35 per cent. A mere 8 per cent of British homes fall into this category, while many Eastern European countries have more privately rented properties than we do.

It was the desire for equity which led the Labour governments of the 1960s and 1970s to introduce laws to protect tenants, by restricting rents and giving security of tenure. The changes were very well intentioned because people had been suffering at the hands of landlords who 'persuaded' their tenants to leave in order to re-let the property at a higher rent. This became known as 'Rachmanism' after a particularly unpleasant exponent of such activities. The unfortunate side-effect of this legislation has been the shrinking supply of private rented accommodation. There are now approximately 550 000 private dwellings standing empty and many others have been sold to owner occupiers, often as a result of the Rent Act.

The law had the effect of putting a price ceiling on rents. Figure 2.3 shows how restricting rents means that fewer landlords will be prepared to make properties available as their rewards will be reduced.

Problems have also arisen because maintenance costs have become very expensive and rents have not been allowed to increase, causing many houses to fall into disrepair. If costs rise but revenue

FIGURE 2.3

The Effect of Rent Control on the Supply of Private Rented Housing

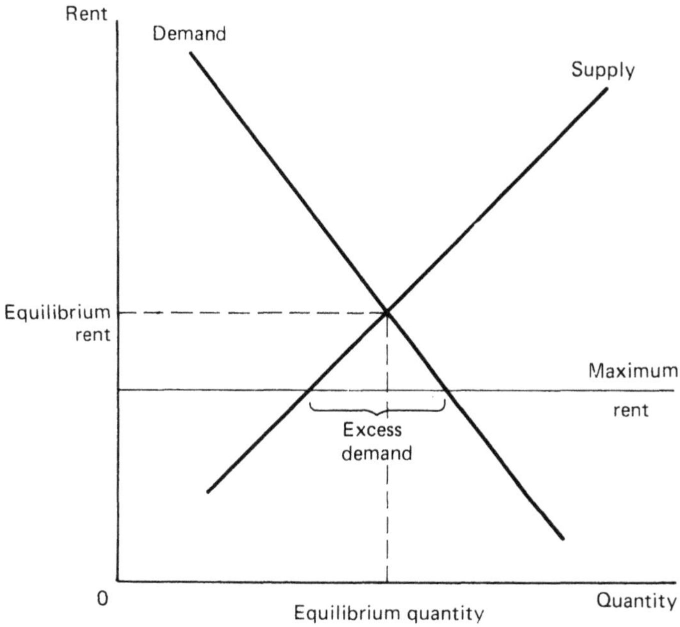

cannot, the profit margin will fall and the incentive to participate in the housing market will be diminished.

The government has introduced legislation to remove some controls from the private rented sector in order to overcome these problems. Tenants will no longer have the same degree of security and landlords will be able to charge market rents instead of 'fair' rents which, under the previous law, were approved on the basis that they would provide a 'reasonable' profit. These gradually fell below normal profit and were an inadequate reward for a landlord who could use his resources more efficiently in other ways. Now rent assessment committees will look at market rents for similar properties and set the amount accordingly. Some commentators suggest that rents will double or treble as a result. The government plans to meet the difference, for those who are unable to pay, through

Housing Benefit but there are fears about the level at which it will be payable.

The only sectors of the rental market that have boomed are hostels and bed and breakfast accommodation. Demand has risen sharply and as there are no price controls the councils that pay the bills are often at the mercy of the owners. The prices set are more akin to hotels than the housing market.

Equity and efficiency are obviously difficult to balance in this field. If the housing market is to be efficient, it must be flexible and able to meet changing demands. The 'manpower crisis' faced by Crawley is not only a result of there being problems in the buying and renting market. Controls on rents and tenancies have led to excess demand and inflexibilities in both the housing and the labour market.

Both these constraints have prevented the economy running efficiently, as developing industries in some areas have faced recruitment problems and their growth has been restricted. A shortage of labour often means that local firms must offer higher wages, so costs rise and industry becomes less competitive.

A security firm has had such problems recruiting staff in the South East that it has taken over a block of flats to house new employees from the North East. Wages are pegged at the level they would have been in the North East but accommodation is free.

Relaxing the restrictions removes some of the protection which has benefited individuals when faced with landlords who have wanted to evict them in order to increase the rent. The government is clearly anticipating an increase in harassment as it is tightening the law to protect the tenant.

Without rental support from government it seems that equity and efficiency are incompatible. The profit motive is necessary to persuade owners to let their property but equity requires that everyone has a decent home despite low incomes. The problem of housing is therefore only part of the greater problem of poverty. If everyone could pay the market rent the problem of sufficient basic housing would disappear as supply would increase. The debate would then move to the speed, location and quality of provision.

Developing Housing Associations

Housing associations have developed significantly in the past thirty years and now represent 3 per cent of the total housing stock. They are organisations which are set up, sometimes by charitable bodies, to provide low-cost housing to rent or sell. They control about 25 per cent of the private rented sector and have been almost the only investor in recent times. Their role in providing low-cost housing has been very important and they have been helped by Housing Association Grants from the government.

The government's policy is to encourage them to attract more private finance to help them to develop further. In order to persuade the private sector to provide finance, rents will have to approach market levels as investors will want to see a reasonable rate of return on their money. The government suggests that rent controls will not be necessary as the availability of grants will enable low-income tenants to cope with this increase. Pressure groups, like the Association of Metropolitan Authorities, fear that this may be the cue for the government to withdraw funding as the private sector becomes more dominant.

However, to encourage the market to work efficiently and provide more housing it is necessary to pay the market rate of return. Once again, we have a situation where efficiency and equity do not seem to work well together. If the market is to form the main source of provision, the state must be prepared to help those who are unable to provide for themselves.

Housing Action Trusts

Housing Action Trusts or HATs are being established to assist in the regeneration of some of the most run-down parts of the inner cities. They will be run by a chairman and members appointed by the secretary of state. HATs will be concerned with the repair, improvement and management of estates of which they have taken control. Their role is not limited to housing as they are also concerned with projects to stimulate economic activity, especially job creation and the provision of better local amenities.

HATs will take over these areas from the local authorities and run them for five years, at the end of which they will hand the houses over to other landlords such as private companies or housing associations. Local authorities which control these inner city areas are worried about the undemocratic nature of these organisations and are concerned about tenants' rights. If these inner city areas are 'gentrified', demand for housing will rise and more affluent residents will move in as house prices and rents increase. Higher price levels alone would increase supply as there would be an incentive to renovate housing that is currently uninhabitable. The local authorities would like more funds to deal with the problem areas themselves.

The Future Demand for Housing

The South East is an area facing increasing pressure to absorb more and more new houses. When most people, especially country dwellers, are asked where these houses should go, their reply has been, 'Not in my back yard!' Having chosen to live in the peace and quiet of rural Britain they do not wish to be disturbed.

This attitude has been seen as selfishness, but objectors from the pressure group Sane Planning in the South East point out that there is more to it. The houses that are being built are not designed to meet local needs but are for well-off commuters. This means that young people in these towns and villages cannot afford to stay there. As more and more people move into the area, the infrastructure is unable to cope, traffic congestion grows, schools and hospitals become overcrowded and the communities become one amorphous urban sprawl. Thus housing determines social development.

The question that such pressure groups ask is, 'Why here?' Places like Milton Keynes, Corby and Peterborough advertise widely in order to attract people and industry, so why not go there? The developers would argue that they are only building houses that people want and that market efficiency demands. This problem is not only associated with rural Britain as the following article shows.

SUBURBS STAND BY TO REPEL BUILDERS

The 'Not in My Back Yard' syndrome appears to be spreading from the shires to the suburbs as a public enquiry opens at Harrow in North London.

The dispute is seen as a test case for incursions into areas previously thought safe from development.

Builders want to demolish 11 detached houses in Elm Park

Road, Pinner, many worth £350,000 and build 20 semis and 80 flats. A further block of houses also appears to be threatened.

In spite of opposition from residents and the Tory MP, Mr Robert Hughes, Harrow council fears the developers will win.

The project meets the government's aim of making fuller use of housing land. The existing houses provide about twenty habitable rooms to the acre, against a borough guideline of 70–100.

One resident said, 'It is difficult to define what we are trying to save. We are talking about character, atmosphere and the quality of the environment which will be destroyed.'

A representative of the Finchley Local Action Group reckons that there are up to three applications a week to build on existing housing sites and back gardens. 'Taken collectively, they are gradually changing the whole face of the borough, and all of London.'

Opposition in outer London boroughs to developers pulling down houses to build 10 or 20 times as many homes has prompted the minister responsible for planning to warn of a backlash unless local planners devise development control practices which reconcile people to house building. Quality of life matters in town too, he said recently.

Adapted from *The Guardian*, 26 September 1988.

The same concerns are voiced by people in both urban and rural communities when their environment is threatened. These fears are very understandable as for most people the greatest investment of their life is buying a house, so any changes which might affect its value will obviously cause anxiety.

Finding new locations to build houses, without upsetting the local residents, is a difficulty which will have to be faced if the economy of the South East is to develop further. The problem of incursions into the green belt round London will be dealt with in Chapter 5, Conservation and the Environment, as it involves other development issues.

The alternative argument relating to development in the South East suggests that as prices rise higher and higher the market mechanism will redirect development to regions where property is cheaper. In the late 1980s this started to happen as prices in and around London stabilised while still rising elsewhere.

Could More Government Spending Help?

In the 1980s, the government laid stress on private sector developments, while cutting the quantity of public housing available. The Labour Party suggests that it would increase house building by about 10 per cent a year which would gradually help those on waiting lists for public sector homes. The most pressing need seems to be to overcome the waste of money involved in short-term housing as this would release millions of pounds to enable new houses to be built.

A combination of private and public sector is a growing solution to the housing shortage. A coalition between developers and local authorities has meant that both sectors have been able to benefit. Councils in some areas, such as London's docklands, have sold land on condition that some public housing will be built on the site.

In every social issue more money will solve the problem but there is always the question of opportunity cost. What do we have to give up?

Until a degree of equity is achieved more money will be needed. The private sector was regarded throughout the 1980s as the best source of extra housing because of its greater efficiency, but unfortunately it does not always serve those who are in the greatest need.

3 Education

It is the obligation of the State to make sure that education is good, that there are high standards and that it is equally available to everybody.

This statement was made by a representative of the education department of Connecticut, then a Republican state, when she was explaining why the market mechanism could not be allowed to dominate the field of education.

Our industrial competitors, whatever their political and cultural differences, have one thing in common. They believe that a strong and successful state education system is synonymous with economic success.

The direct implications of the quotation seem to be about equity and concern the individual, as it suggests that the state has an obligation to provide equality of opportunity in education for all its citizens. The level of education is often the single factor which determines how people will spend the rest of their lives as it influences lifetime earnings and therefore quality of life. Figure 3.2, later in the chapter, demonstrates the difference between a graduate's and a non-graduate's earning stream. A similar effect is observable in comparing all standards of education. In fact the earnings of those with the poorest education tend to reach a peak in the middle of their working life and fall towards retirement. There are therefore considerable private benefits to be gained from education.

The ultimate measure of equality would be freedom of access, when everyone who is willing and able can receive as much education as they want. Limited resources mean that this aim cannot usually be met. Instead, the view that no one should be denied a 'minimum quantity' of education is often adopted. In Britain, this is interpreted as free education until 18. Beyond this point it is means tested.

The Benefits of Education

Resources devoted to education are investment, just as building a factory is investment. Both are adding to the future productive capacity of the country. People are just another form of capital, often known as human capital. Production benefits therefore result from the effective provision of education. A well-educated population tends to be a more productive workforce. Optimising the available resources means that everyone should be educated in such a way that they can use their abilities to the full. Research has shown that the level of both general and vocational education affects productivity. Despite Britain's level of economic growth, it appears that productivity is increasing faster in some European countries whose education systems are more far reaching. Some of these are investigated later in the chapter.

The level of education is reflected in the ability of the population to make the most of other forms of government provision. These positive externalities of education funding make spending in areas like health, employment, transport and many others more effective as people will be able to use them with greater understanding. As these effects make society function more efficiently, they are known as social benefits. All decision-making, both social and economic, is helped by a good education.

Educating for Change

Today's workforce faces much greater demands than their counterparts in the past. On leaving school a young man was likely to start a career that he would continue for the rest of his life, but this is no longer so. Flexibility has become the key to ongoing employment in the later decades of the twentieth century. The role of the five-year apprenticeship has become obsolete in many fields as the development of new techniques means that constant retraining is necessary. The skills that have been learnt may become redundant as technology changes and results in pools of unemployed people who have to be retrained.

In order to provide the country with a workforce that can cope with these changing requirements everyone must receive a sound general education. In developed countries it is difficult to separate the effects of education to 16 as almost 100 per cent of the population has received ten or eleven years of schooling in the post-war period. However, work which has been done in developing countries, where groups who receive differing amounts of education can be more readily identified, suggests that a good general education provides a high level of both social and private returns. In this environment, higher education added far more to private returns than social returns. It seems likely that in more developed societies the most effective level of education would be somewhat higher in order to cope with the complexities of modern living.

The role of vocational training has come into question because it may provide people with skills but no jobs as technology changes. To overcome this problem a broad education is necessary to give people flexibility between areas of the same trade.

The French system of training for the building industry aims to provide this breadth of training. The course for brickwork, for example, deals with concrete as well and also includes skills in making the wooden shapes to receive concrete and fixing steel rods for reinforcement. In Britain, these are regarded as separate skills and the basic course simply deals with brickwork. Students attend full time at vocational schools whereas in Britain most students are part time on day release from work. Not only is the course broader but students are expected to pass exams in maths, legislation and economics, and French as well as lengthy practical assessment. In Germany, the system for qualification as a craftsman is very similar.

Foremen in Britain tend to have got the job after years of experience on the shop-floor but have no further qualifications. In Germany, almost all foremen have passed an exam to become a 'Meister'.

A Meister must be able to carry out routine setting and maintenance of machines, show the ability to cope with supervising staff, organise work efficiently and carry out repairs to machines. This provides him with skills which are designed to make his section in the factory work more efficiently. The effects are evident from the differing levels of productivity found in similar factories in the two countries. The main cause of difference was the ability of the foreman to repair faults. In the British factory production stopped until the maintenance crew arrived as such work was not part of the foreman's remit. Efficient supervision and an appreciation of the needs of the workforce will also lead to higher output.

It seems that education, both general and vocational, is fundamental to improving economic growth and productivity and that we have some lessons to learn from our European neighbours about how to make the most of our resources.

Education, like other services provided by the government, could absorb all the money available and a lot more. As a result choices have to be made about the level and type of provision. To make an informed choice the government must have some idea of what it gets for its money, but in fact little is known about which combination of resources gives the best results. There are two alternative approaches to try to solve this problem.

Cost–Benefit Analysis

Cost–benefit analysis has been used by industry and governments to decide whether certain investment projects will provide a reasonable level of return. By adding up all the costs and all the benefits a comparison can be made. In areas like education such decision-making is more complex as the costs and benefits are more difficult to calculate than in a road-building scheme for example. Cost–benefit analysis can be used more effectively when investigating individual projects than in deciding levels of spending in general. It has been used widely by aid-giving organisations like the World Bank to assess the relative merits of alternative uses for their funds. In the developing world, where education is in short supply, the private benefits resulting from even a small amount can be considerable. The first step on the ladder provides access to higher stages and is often the path to a new way of life. In weighing up alternative ways of spending money, the donor agencies will be more interested in the external effects of educating people. This may be the provision of more doctors, teachers, engineers or other skilled personnel who will help the country to become more self-sufficient. They will be anxious at the prospect of recently qualified recruits making the most of their new skills and leaving the country for a more affluent lifestyle elsewhere. Private benefit will then be the only gain.

Counting the costs

This is the easy part of the exercise. The costs of teachers, buildings, books and chalk are simple addition sums and the total figures are available in central and local government accounts. These are all private costs and can be measured by the market as there is a price attached to each item. Allocating some of these costs to individual institutions is more of a problem as the cost of shared resources, such as field study centres and back up facilities for teachers, have to be apportioned. The capital costs and running costs must also be shared out.

Balancing the benefits

The question that has to be answered is 'What benefits do we include?' Education provides us with all sorts of benefits, from enabling us to pass Economics exams to helping us to fit in with the rest of the community. It might be possible to put some sort of monetary value on an exam result if it helps us to get a job or a place in higher education. This may have a direct effect on our future career path and lifetime earnings. Learning to live with other people is also very useful, to them as well as us. It is a shared, social benefit and as such is much more difficult to calculate. It is also an intangible without any market price to reflect its exchange value.

On this wider scale, we need to assess the benefits the whole economy will derive from education. The government pays millions of pounds each year to fund education but the benefits do not become apparent until those students emerge into the world of work. So it has to be remembered that in education spending benefits are often deferred both for the state and the individual. Education is, therefore, a long-term investment.

The question must also be asked, whether costs and benefits can always be looked at from a purely economic point of view. Local newspapers in many parts of the country have produced headlines like this:

'Village School Under Threat of Closure'

The reaction in the village is violent opposition as they fear that a focal point of their community will disappear. Their children, from the age of 5, will have to get a bus at crack of dawn to a large school far away.

The education authority claims that the school is not viable on both economic and educational grounds. The economic reasons are true enough. It costs a lot more to run several small schools than one large one.

A small village school will need proportionately more teachers per pupil as there will be fewer children in each age group. In Norfolk, schools of fifty to sixty pupils have three teachers, forty pupils would entitle them to two whereas urban schools have a ratio of 27.5 pupils to each teacher plus a head teacher. Large schools mean economies of scale as the fixed costs are spread over more pupils so local

FIGURE 3.1
Economies of Scale: Small School Versus Large School

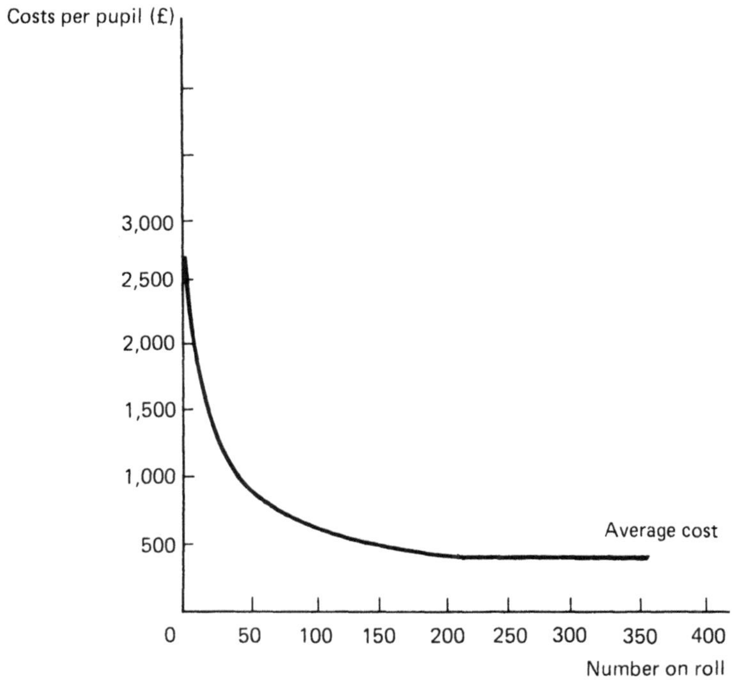

authorities save money. There are all sorts of costs in the provision of a school that do not vary according to its size. It is difficult to employ half a caretaker or have half a central heating boiler (small ones aren't half the price of large ones). These fixed costs do not change as the school gets larger. It is therefore cheaper to run a large school than a small one as the cost curve in Figure 3.1 shows.
The data come from Devon, where they have worked out the costs of schools of different sizes:

Number on roll	*Cost per pupil*
14	£2669
30	£1060
50	£839
350	£578

The range is enormous and people in towns might justifiably question the disproportionate spending on these children.

The educational costs arise because of the limited experience that may be available for the children. A school with fourteen children is restricted to the skills of its two teachers. Many activities are impossible with so small a number. It cannot even stage a decent football match.

On both grounds the Minister of Education decided that all schools with three teachers or less should close. This announcement caused uproar as people realised the implications. It would mean the closure of a total of 1900 schools in England and Wales. It was not just parents that were objecting but many counties as well. They were concerned about the complex web of social, community, geographical and educational factors which make the village school an integral part of village life. On this occasion the ballyhoo worked, the minister withdrew the death sentence.

The additional cost of running village schools had been accepted because of the benefits they provide for the community. However, the problems of their restricted scope still remained. Economics was applied once again. Schools have been linked together in clusters so that they can share scarce resources, both physical and human. Children from several schools would be brought together to benefit from the varied skills of individual teachers and the use of specialist equipment. Even a game of football becomes viable. The government has backed the initiative by providing educational support grants to enable these schemes to get off the ground.

Input–Output Analysis

Profit-maximising firms always look for the best possible combination of resources to make each output level of their products. This involves testing different proportions of inputs to see which produces the best result. The data which is produced is known as a production function. More recently, this principle has been applied to education but it is not nearly as straightforward because neither inputs nor outputs are so easily measured.

- The inputs into a school are the land, labour and capital which are used. In other words, the site it is built on, the staff who run it and all the buildings and equipment used in it. But there is more to it than simply figures. The background of students and aspects of the teaching staff as well as how the money is spent will all influence the effectiveness of a school. The same combination of inputs may have different effects in different places.
- The most common way of measuring outputs is to look at exam results. The National Curriculum, introduced for the 1990s, depends on and develops this approach. This, of course, is the easiest way to approach the problem but most schools and colleges would claim a wider role such as character development and personal relationships. But these objectives are much harder to measure so researchers have avoided them and work has been carried out on the basis of external exam results or other forms of testing.

The aim of input–output analysis is to measure economic efficiency, in other words, how to achieve certain objectives at the lowest cost. It has been used widely in developing countries to assist decision-making about using money most effectively in the provision of education. It is now developing a more important role in Britain as government spending has come under critical review.

Education, like other service industries, finds it difficult to improve productivity. A hairdresser may be able to increase the number of clients seen in a day, but if quality falls and customers don't feel that they are getting the same level of service they will go elsewhere. Improving productivity may mean that class sizes rise but it is generally accepted that small classes give students greater opportunities. It therefore seems that it is difficult to make the teaching staff more productive without lowering standards.

There seem to be two approaches to improving the value that the government gets from education spending. One is to make the current system more efficient, another is to persuade others to invest in education. The current government is attempting to develop the funding of education along both these lines. In making the system more efficient it is trying to provide a workforce which is more suited to the current needs of the economy.

Until recently all state schools have been funded directly by local authorities. The amount of money that they receive has depended on the views of the local authority and factors such as the number of pupils in the school. There has been special help available for schools in Educational Priority Areas where there are many social problems. In trying to meet the two objectives mentioned above a variety of schemes has been proposed, some have proved viable but others are still under consideration.

Vouchers: The Market at Work

Freedom of choice is one of the fundamental principles of the market. In most of our purchases we exercise this freedom, but in education the options are more restricted. Governments have always advocated that parents should be able to choose but in reality this choice has been limited by the facilities available. The 1944 Education Act qualified the element of choice with the following words: 'so far as is compatible with the provision of efficient instruction and training and the avoidance of unreasonable public expenditure'.

This, of course, placed few constraints on the actions of governments and local authorities. Pupils could be refused entry to a school if there simply wasn't room or, equally, if the number of students in each school became unbalanced, so that the costs per head rose in half-empty schools.

Vouchers seemed to be the perfect solution to the problem as it put choice firmly in the hands of the consumers. They are simply a piece of paper which represents a year's worth of education. The value may vary according to the age of the child and they may be 'spent' wherever the parents wish, in a private or state school.

There has been much debate over the pros and cons of such schemes.

Advocates of vouchers claim that the system gives more freedom of choice and brings private education within the scope of people who otherwise couldn't afford it. They argue that it overcomes the inequity of people paying twice, through taxation and school fees. If each individual could select the school they wanted their child to attend, market forces would be allowed to work because no one would want bad schools so these would contract while the good ones grew.

Critics, on the other hand, object because public money would be fed into the private sector and there would be less available for state education. If unpopular schools are left with few pupils resources will be wasted. Popular schools simply cannot expand during the summer holidays to meet the needs of a growing intake. Their final point is more difficult to evaluate: popularity may not be synonymous with a good education. A smart uniform can sometimes be misleading.

A survey was carried out in Ashford by Kent County Council which showed that the results might not have been as startling as either side thought.

- 12 per cent of parents would have chosen a different school
- 7 per cent more would have opted for the private sector

Even relatively small percentage changes like this have considerable cost implications as more children would be travelling further to school and some would be leaving the public sector. The main constraint is that the system will only work if there is surplus capacity in the schools which are in demand. Chris Patten, when he was deputy Secretary of State for Education, summed them up as being 'theoretically interesting' but 'practically hopeless', but they may yet be brought into the arena for future discussion.

In general, the people who would gain from vouchers are the well-informed members of society who would be able to use the system to their benefit. Recently, a quite different application of the voucher idea has been suggested which would attempt to even out society's inequalities. It involves providing vouchers of unequal value so most help goes to the poor while the wealthy receive less. From the point of view of reallocating wealth and opportunity it seems a good idea but faces all sorts of problems in its application. How do you decide how much each family is entitled to? The means test is a dirty word as it is difficult to implement and regarded as unfair. Perhaps zones according to house value might be the answer, but areas tend not to be totally uniform so money would be given to rich and poor alike.

The problems associated with social inequality are not always based on money. In working a market system like this people need considerable skills to make the most of it. This might mean that the least capable would suffer more than when their fate was left to the state.

STUDENTS PREPARE TO EARN THEIR KEEP

Sweeping changes to make students pay towards their upkeep will be proposed by the government this week.

The measures will include interest free loans of up to £400 a year, a freeze on grants and an easing of the financial burden on parents.

They will be followed by a controversial 'earn-as-you-learn' initiative designed to provide paid employment for undergraduates during term time. They will be expected to increase their income by volunteering to clean college windows, mow lawns and work in campus libraries. This will be the first step in the gradual shift to the American system of self-reliance.

The government's loan scheme, due to be introduced from September 1990, will subsidise the cost of borrowing to enable loans to be interest free as opposed to the 13 per cent students are currently charged for loans and overdrafts. The loans will be linked to inflation. It will also underwrite all loans. Loans will be made in three roughly equal annual instalments to prevent students getting heavily into debt by the end of their first year. Initially, they will be barred from borrowing more than about £400 in any one year, well below the figure originally considered. Eventually they will form the main part of a student's financial support.

Students will not have to start paying the money back until after they graduate, and only after their salaries rise above a 'trigger' threshold. This safeguard will ensure graduates are not deterred from entering the lower paid professions.

Alister Macrae, a national secretary for the National Union for Public Employees, has attacked using students as 'cheap labour'. 'We would resist it most strongly,' he said. Students attending an institution should concentrate completely on the course they are on. That is their prime responsibility.'

Adapted from *The Sunday Times*, 6 October 1988

Grants v. Loans

Since 1962 local authorities have had to give grants to students studying for degrees. The amount of the state's contribution has varied according to the income of a student's parents. Neither the amount of the grant nor the level of income at which it is payable has risen in line with inflation, so not only has the total grant diminished in real value but parents have had to pay a larger and larger proportion of it.

The rising cost of education has led the government to investigate whether there is a more efficient way of funding students. The debate between loans and grants has continued for a long time but reached a head in 1988 when, for the first time, firm proposals were made.

In Britain the level of support for students has been more generous than probably anywhere else in the world. Student loans are common in most of Western Europe and North America. In countries that give grants, such as Sweden, they are usually of much lower value.

Equity is an argument which is used by protagonists on both sides of the case. Those who are in favour of loans will argue that it is unfair on the taxpayer to provide the finance for students to receive an education which will raise their future income stream well above the average (Figure 3.2).

The argument is reinforced when the social groupings of students is compared with the population as a whole. Approximately two-thirds of the population are categorised as 'working class' whereas four-fifths of all students in higher education are regarded as 'middle class'.

These facts are interpreted quite differently by those who argue that grants should be continued and increased. The reason that there are so few working-class students in higher education is that the short-run opportunity cost of three years at university is the wages that they have to give up and the extra drain on their families as full grants cease at relatively low levels. The introduction of loans would make such an investment even less acceptable as it would involve a commitment to repay a debt over many years when they first start work.

If loans proved to be to be a deterrent, the country would be depriving itself of a large sector of the people it needs to help future

FIGURE 3.2
The Costs and Benefits of Higher Education

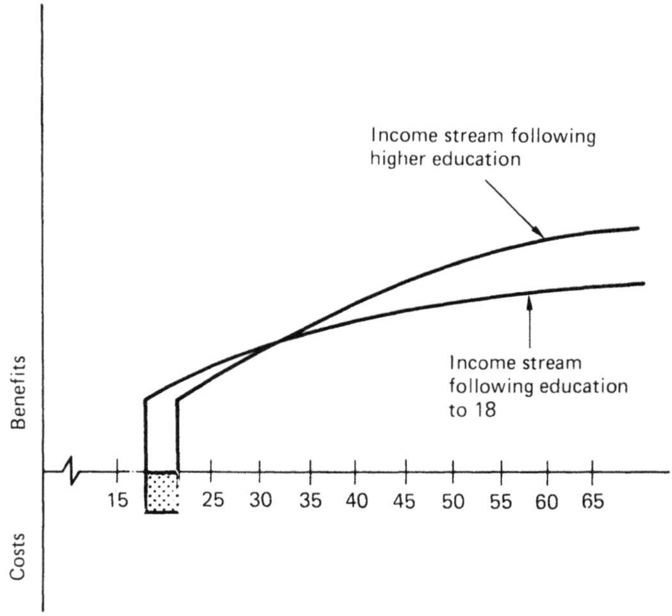

growth and development. In the USA, loan schemes have been running for some time and do not appear to have been a deterrent, but attitudes in America do tend to differ.

A loan scheme may not be a cheap option for the government as all countries which run them have found that the cost has been much greater than expected. Inflation always affects lenders negatively as the real value of repayments falls. The sheer number of students will cause a great administrative burden and there is always a fair proportion who fail to keep their side of the agreement. Low interest rates are usually part of the package and this is a subsidy which must be borne by the government.

If higher education were left to the market, the student would have to meet the full cost. The lifetime earnings flow shows that it is worthwhile as a long-term investment as the private benefits are great. This is perhaps an example of people not making a rational choice because they have imperfect information. If the market were the sole means of provision, the range of courses taken up would be limited to those which had good investment value for the individual in the economy.

What Is Fair?

The simple answer to this question is that it depends who you are. If we look at it from the point of view of the individual, different schemes have different benefits.

Until the new British scheme is introduced it will be difficult to evaluate its effect. Will it mean that the government will have more money to expand higher education because less will be paid out in grants? Will it mean that fewer working-class students will go on to higher education for fear of burdening themselves with a loan for the next ten or twenty years? Will the cost of implementing the scheme outweigh the financial benefits to the state?

FIGURE 3.3
Grants and Loans: Who Wins?

		Why?
UK	Best for the good student	Grants for the élite
US	Best for the average, non-standard or part-time student	Loans readily available
Sweden	Best for the parent	No financial burden
		Small grants/large loan
France	Best for the taxpayer	Small grants according to means

Sponsorship

Industry has, for a long time, been involved in providing financial help for education. Many large companies such as BP, Shell and Unilever have played a role in funding educational developments. The government has, in the late 1980s, looked for a more formal and more lucrative tie between the two sectors through the development of City Technology Colleges and Compacts. The university and polytechnic sector is now seeking money from industry to finance research and development projects. Industry has a growing incentive for involvement in education because in the 1990s the numbers joining the labour market will fall rapidly, so firms will have to work hard to attract young employees.

The changing structure of British industry means that there is an increasing demand for people with expertise in science and technology. At present, supply exceeds demand in many other fields, so the government decided to develop a new type of school aiming to

The Benefits

The CTC initiative will improve standards in urban areas and increase parental choice. CTCs will be at the leading edge of curriculum development in science and technology and will pioneer new approaches to school management. They will provide opportunities for industry and commerce, the providers of future employment, to influence the education process at a far earlier stage than is currently the case. The achievements of CTCs will be widely imitated.

Conservative Party
Keynote Brief

- More money coming into education
- Students with the skills industry needs
- More parental choice
- Improve standards of education in urban areas
- Stimulate development in teaching science and technology

The Costs

The effect the schools are likely to have on the surrounding area is central. The CTC argument is that these will act as beacons of excellence which will force other schools to pull themselves up. It's a market argument and assumes fair competition and the competition is plainly not fair but is so loaded that were these institutions making widgets rather than selling education, they would go before the Office of Fair Trading because the market has been rigged.

Jack Straw
Labour Party Education Spokesman

Critics of the scheme base their arguments on the negative externalities or costs which the development of CTCs will create for other schools serving this age group.

- There are fewer students of this age so roles are falling in most schools. Providing more schools means that costs rise as students are spread more thinly or other schools have to close as they haven't enough students.
- Teachers of Science and Technology will be tempted to leave other schools because of better resources in CTCs. Standards of teaching in these areas will fall for the rest of the population.
- The best pupils will want to go to CTCs because of their facilities. Standards will fall elsewhere.
- The total amount of money being spent could go a long way to helping schools in general.

provide an education which emphasised these skills. It looked to industry for financial support to establish them.

The plan was greeted with varying degrees of enthusiasm. Some firms felt that their own endeavours were a better use of money, while others contributed generously. High street names such as Boots, W. H. Smith, Dixons, Marks & Spencer and the Hanson Trust have all been involved, some contributing up to £1 million.

The government and those firms which are participating in the scheme have looked at the benefits of City Technology Colleges, but educationalists have been more concerned with the costs that have been incurred and the effect on the rest of the education system.

Compacts

This scheme, which has been greeted with more enthusiasm, is designed to bring schools and industry together so that they can provide for each others needs more successfully. Compacts are an agreement in which industry provides resources to train and encourage school children. Schools undertake to support the scheme and pupils agree to improve their standards. They are mainly centred on inner city areas where there is a skills' mismatch between school leavers and the jobs available. The implications and effects of Compacts will be investigated later, in the chapter looking at inner cities.

The Future

There are two significant areas of change with which the education system must come to grips if it is to rise to the challenge of the 1990s.

The changing economic structure means that workers need to be both skilled and flexible. The declining number of school leavers requires every individual to make the maximum contribution during their working life.

To achieve the greatest possible return from education, we must encourage more students to continue their studies in order to make the most of their abilities and provide industry with the type of employees it needs. The 'staying-on' rate has been very poor in Britain compared with other developed countries and its growth rate has been slower.

Education must also be an ongoing process. A sample of workers in Sweden were asked if they had taken part in any form of education in the past year. Fifty-eight per cent of professional workers, 54 per cent of white collar workers and 43 per cent of unskilled workers said they had. The courses they follow are designed to refresh and update their knowledge and this helps the

TABLE 3.1
Who Stays On? (per cent)

Country	*1970–71*	*1983–84*
West Germany	33	62
France	63	79
Italy	47	72
Netherlands	60	92
Belgium	66	83
Luxembourg	43	58
UK	**42**	**53**
Ireland	55	77
Denmark	45	90
Greece	51	48
Average	48	68

country adapt to changing needs. Its GDP per head is one and a half times the EC average.

In order to overcome the problems created by structural change we must first encourage more students to stay at school, but secondly, we must ensure that the nature of their education will provide both them and the country with an asset which will facilitate a flexible approach to future development. Labour, an increasingly scarce resource, must be used efficiently.

Health: Who Waits, Who Pays? 4

PRISONER OF PURSE-STRINGS

Doctors in Wolverhampton had some rare good news last week. They heard the town's hospitals were to get £209 000 from the government's £100m health service cash injection. It is enough for administrators to risk reopening the 28-bed ward they shut last month.

But the money is not enough to open any of the other 58 beds that are shut at the Royal; or the 39 gynaecological and orthopaedic beds that are out of action at the New Cross. Nor will it help the 30 bed Penn children's hospital that Wolverhampton closed as part of its savings programme earlier this month.

The shortage – almost one in six of the beds at the two hospitals are closed – has dramatically increased pressure on medical staff and patients. At the Royal, an elderly building in the centre of town, a few casualty admissions is enough to trip the hospital's delicately balanced allocation of beds, sending administrative staff and doctors scouring the wards, begging beds from different departments and discharging patients.

'There's been a chronic bed shortage in Wolverhampton for some time,' says Steve Connellan, one of the doctors at New Cross. 'Now we are so short of beds that even with increased efficiency we are worried that patients will not get an emergency bed or will be discharged too early.'

Now, still needing cuts to balance the budget, Wolverhampton can guarantee only that an efficient emergency and urgent service will be maintained. For people here, anything on top, where there is no immediate threat to life is a bonus.

Adapted from *The Sunday Times*, 24 January 1988

FIGURE 4.1
Spending on the NHS in England

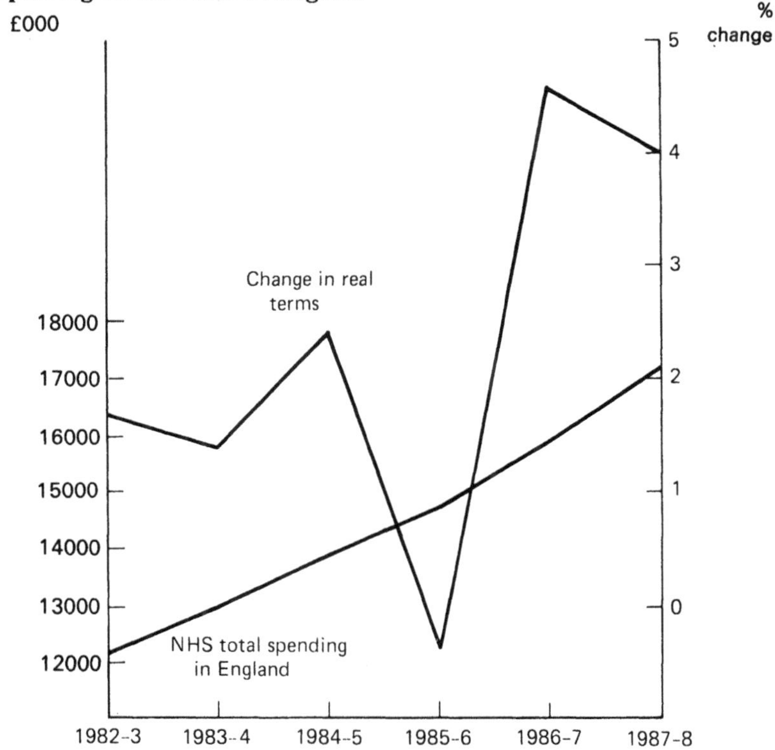

SOURCE: House of Commons, Social Services Committee 1986–87, *Public Expenditure on Social Services* (HMSO, 1987).

Why Is There a Problem?

More money than ever before is being spent on the National Health Service (Figure 4.1) so why do problems still exist? Hospitals throughout the country are facing shortages of funds in many vital areas. The provision of medical care in the community is still being cut back despite the fact that that there has been a real increase in the funding available. The 1980s have seen health spending rise more than 30 per cent faster than the general retail price index.

One problem is that the rate of inflation in the health service has been substantially greater than in the economy as a whole. Wages represent 70 per cent of total costs and they have risen faster than inflation elsewhere. In order to maintain standards, therefore, even more funding is needed.

TABLE 4.1
Has Spending Power Really Increased by 30 per cent?

	1982–3	*1983–4*	*1984–5*	*1985–6*	*1986–7*	*1987–8*
% increase in spending	9.1	5.9	7.4	5.8	7.7	8.7
Health service inflation %	7.4	5.0	5.9	5.4	6.5	
Change in purchasing power %	1.5	0.9	1.3	0.3	1.1	

SOURCE: *Public Expenditure on Social Services* (HMSO, 1987).

The data show the extent of the problem. Far from having 30 per cent more to spend, the health authorities have had to cope with an average increase in funding of approximately 1 per cent each year. But the demand for health services has grown faster than this supply.

Standard of living is a crucial factor in determining the demand for health care. As people become better off they expect an improved service and are less prepared to put up with ailments that might previously have been regarded as a minor inconvenience. Equally, the reverse is also true. An increase in the rate of unemployment has also been shown to put greater pressure on medical resources, as being without a job causes much stress. The following statistics reflect this increase in demand.

TABLE 4.2
The Number of Patients Treated in England (thousands)

	1978	*1986*	%
In-patients cases	5370	6414	19
Day cases	562	1050	87
Out-patients attendances	33 950	37 728	11

SOURCE: Conservative Central Office, *Politics Today*, 13 Nov–1 Oct 1987.

Constant innovation is another factor which has caused the demand curve for health to shift to the right. Recent developments in health care have meant that more people can be cured and more people can be kept alive longer than ever before. Heart transplants and other forms of advanced medical care are extremely expensive, but have two roles. First, they maintain life, which is the prime concern, of course. Secondly, they offer research and development to allow further advances to be made. This, in turn, makes the bill for the National Health Service grow at an increasing rate.

Individual demand for major medical care is inelastic. Not many people would volunteer to have their appendixes removed or their kidneys replaced if it wasn't absolutely necessary. The constant discovery of new techniques maintains the inelasticity but increases the level of demand.

Britain has an ageing population. The average cost of health care for the elderly is naturally higher than for the population as a whole, so once again the demands on the health budget are rising. The combination of an increasing number of old people and new techniques for lengthening life combine to create demands that are very expensive to meet. The government has committed itself to certain priority aims such as the development of home kidney treatment and community care which are all, once again, additions to the total bill.

Large sectors of the British economy have met targets of increasing demand through increasing productivity. The health service faces a problem because it is very labour intensive and productivity is difficult to improve. Nurses, physiotherapists and others need to spend time with patients in order to give them acceptable medical care. It seems impossible to substitute machinery for people as they are unable to perform the human side of the work.

The management structure of the National Health Service has been subjected to much criticism. If administration is inefficient it will eat up a high proportion of the funds available and therefore reduce the resources which could be used for patient care. This has been one of the main focuses of reform in recent years, in fact £400 million have been released by efficiency drives.

The fundamental problems of the health service relate to the increase in demand, the increase in supply of new techniques and the problems of financing all aspects of this proliferation. Overall, therefore, the NHS would need to grow around 2 per cent a year to meet the expanding demands. This is twice the rate of increase of its actual resources.

Is Health Care Important?

Governments generally regard health care as important. They may argue about how it is provided and its rank order against other calls on their money, but they would agree on some basic principles. Quite simply, a healthy population is a more productive population. In Britain, workers lose 20 days per year for illness, the French lose 14.9, whereas in the United States the figure falls to 4.9.

The provision of health services also leads to a reduced demand for remedial care. The external effect of providing vaccinations, for example, is the elimination of certain infectious diseases, so that more people are protected than those who are actually vaccinated and the total costs of care will subsequently fall. Government policies on screening fall into the same category. If many diseases are discovered in their early stages, treatments are cheaper and more effective, so there are social as well as economic benefits to be gained. Another role of the National Health Service is public education, now increasingly important in the fight against heart disease, one of Britain's major killers. Government spending is therefore not totally altruistic as it may lead to falling demand at a later stage.

Beyond this economic externality, however, there is a wider social function. Health care directly combats personal suffering. In terms of human sympathy, therefore, every case should be treated regardless of cost. In order to do this, what else would we have to give up? Spending on everything else? The following quotation comes from the report of the Royal Commission on the National Health Service which came out in 1979. 'We had no difficulty in believing the proposition put to us by one medical witness that "we can easily spend the whole of the gross national product" ' (Cmnd 7615, July 1979).

Choices have to be made about the allocation of our scarce resources as there are many demands on an inevitably limited supply. Like all other social issues, health care has to come to terms with balancing equity and efficiency.

How Does the British System Work?

The National Health Service was established with the fundamental principle of free access for all, according to need rather than income, in order to achieve equity. It is paid for through taxation which is collected by central government. In fact, in 1988 the average family paid £31 a week, or £1600 a year to the service.

The government runs most of the hospitals and employs most of the doctors and other personnel required to maintain the health service. It controls the quality of the staff by demanding that they should have acceptable qualifications resulting from recognised courses of study which are provided by the state health service.

Medical care is, as a result, freely available to the whole population. There is no charge for a visit to the general practitioner or a stay in hospital. Charges are made for prescriptions, eye tests and dental care but these are generally heavily subsidised and children, the elderly and the very poor are exempt from such payments.

The NHS is organised through area health authorities which are funded by central government according to need. For example, the direction of funding changed when it was realised that provision in the South East far outstripped the facilities available in less well endowed parts of the country.

Despite the development of a system which was designed to ensure equal access to health care for the whole population, there is evidence to suggest that this is not being achieved. More affluent sectors of society seem to get more than their fair share of health care compared to their poorer counterparts. The bottom socio-economic groups receive 40 per cent less National Health Service expenditure than the top groups. There is a variety of reasons for this disparity of which the most important is probably related to pay. Professionals, employers and managers are unlikely to lose money if they take time off work to visit the doctor, whereas manual workers who are paid by the hour or output usually do. It is also more difficult for the lower groups to make an appointment in the first place as they are less likely to have a telephone or a car. They may be faced with poorer provision in the areas where they live so they have to travel further to receive the treatment that they need.

There is a growing private sector in the British health care industry, although it is still only half the size of those in France and Germany and represents less than 1 per cent of GDP. Approximately 10 per cent of the population is covered by private health insurance, a figure which has increased more rapidly since the mid-1970s, as more firms and trade unions offer cover as part of their package. A total of 400 000 operations are carried out every year in private hospitals which accounts for a quarter of all non-urgent medical care, 25 per cent of hip replacement operations and 20 per cent of heart surgery.

The problems of the NHS can be summed up by their waiting lists. Demand is inelastic for many treatments and supply is inadequate so the service is rationed by queuing instead of by price. The queue ensures that effective demand equals supply. Reducing the list would be expensive as it would mean providing more resources. Cutting it to nil would imply that the NHS should always have spare capacity which would cost even more. In an ideal situation the marginal cost of cutting waiting lists would be equal to the marginal benefit which results. The benefits include the well being of the patient as well as other external factors. A hip replacement operation may make an elderly person mobile again, so he or she no longer relies on social services to the same extent. The cost of waiting must, therefore, take into account costs other than pain and inconvenience. The cost of support services is high but has to be met for as long as people are waiting.

If queues are to be reduced, in theory, supply must be increased. Between 1949 and the late 1980s, spending on the NHS has increased from 3.927 to 6.17 per cent of GNP but waiting lists have risen by almost the same proportion. As the system provides new treatments, there are more waiting lists to join.

Do Other Countries Do Better?

Different countries use different approaches to the allocation of resources in the field of health. Sometimes this results from contrasting philosophies whereas in other areas practices for delivering medical care have developed in different ways.The outcome is that the contributions from the public and private sectors vary considerably. The level of provision also varies although this may not

TABLE 4.3
International Comparisons

	United Kingdom	*United States*	*France*
Health-expenditure per head	£653	£809	£941
Health expenditure as a % of GDP (Public)	5.3	4.4	6.5
(Private)	0.6	6.3	2.6
Life expectancy (years) (Male)	71.3	70.9	70.9
(Female)	77.3	78.4	79.1
Infant mortality per thousand (Male)	12.2	12.8	11.2
(Female)	9.4	10.2	8.2
Number of people per hospital bed	124	169	90
Number of people per physician	775	498	480
% of population admitted to hospital p.a.	12.7	17.0	12.1
Average length of stay (days)	18.6	9.9	14.1
Hospital occupancy rates	81.4	78.6	73.2
Nurses per bed occupied	1.09	1.23	0.26

SOURCE: King's Fund Centre, 1987.

correlate with the end result. Men, for example, live longer in Britain despite lower levels of health spending and America's infant mortality figures do not reflect expenditure.

International comparisons are not, however, as straightforward as they might seem (Table 4.3). In order to make such judgements it is important to look at the social structure of a country. From GNP statistics a country may appear to be very rich but the allocation of this wealth may be unequal. People with an inadequate diet, who may have missed out on personal or health education and are perhaps unemployed are less likely to live a long time, and their children are more likely to suffer high infant mortality rates.

Clinical practices also vary from country to country. A decision to treat a patient with drugs rather than an operation will have a significant effect on the final bill. In most cases, a surgical remedy is a great deal more expensive as it generally involves longer hospitalisation, fees to surgeons, anaesthetists and other support services.

USA

The majority of people in the USA are covered by private health insurance.The 13 million self-employed provide their own individual schemes and two-thirds of the population are protected and funded through their employment. Group policies which are provided by firms are the cheapest form of cover.

The old and the poor are helped by government schemes. Medicare is designed to help the 30 million elderly, but it only covers 40 per cent of the cost of any treatment, so it is essential to have insurance or enough savings to pay the remaining 60 per cent. Medicaid is for those whose earnings are below the poverty line. About 22 million people, mainly in family groups, fall into this category.

This leaves 37 million people who have no cover at all. The alternatives, if they fall ill, are to turn to charity or face bankruptcy. Most of this group are the working poor and their families who simply cannot afford or do not arrange insurance premiums but earn just above the limit for Medicaid, so they fall into the poverty trap. Many of these people are unskilled workers in the service sector where pay is low and there is little provision of health insurance.

For those who can pay, the American system is excellent. Competition leads to quality as patients who are not satisfied will find another doctor and hospitals will compete to have the latest equipment. The price mechanism works well for those with the income to afford the prices. Others do less well.

Social problems stemming from this lack of equity are numerous and self-perpetuating. The children of families who can't or won't pay, suffer from ill health and therefore they are set on the downward path of the cycle of deprivation. A child who starts life in this sort of environment will find it difficult to make the most of education, so its prospects in the world of work will be limited. In the long run the next generation will be faced with the same dilemma, hence the term 'cycle'.

The American government has other worries about the provision of health care. The system is extremely expensive. Eleven per cent of America's Gross National Product is already consumed by the private and public sector together. If growth continues at the present rate this will have risen to 15 per cent by the year 2000, which is equivalent to $5550 per person per year. Such a rate of growth far outstrips economic growth and therefore means sacrifices in other areas.

A major cause of increasing costs is that the insurance system leads to inflated charges. In Britain, we find that a garage's attitude to repairing a damaged car is very different if the insurance company is paying! The bill will be considerably larger than usual. The same thing is happening in the American health industry. Doctors use many techniques for increasing their rewards. They may overprescribe drugs or perform unnecessary operations which the insurance company will end up paying for. An American baby is twice as likely as a British baby to be born by Caesarean section. As the doctor is the person who makes the clinical decisions and also writes the bill for the insurance company, it is difficult to question what has been done. A garage will have to wait for an inspector to look at a car that needs repairing before it goes ahead and mends it, but you can't insist that someone with appendicitis waits for the inspector!

The American habit of litigation is also responsible for pushing up costs. Doctors will avoid taking risks as they may be sued if anything goes wrong. Malpractice insurance may cost an American obstetrician $72 000 per year so fees tend to rise to cover the premiums.

France

France has a state run health system, Le Secu, which was established in 1945 and covers much the same areas as Britain's welfare state. It is funded by compulsory contributions from both employers and employees who make payments in a ratio of approximately two to one. The amount collected is calculated as a percentage of income and deducted directly from wages.

When people visit the doctor in France they must pay the fee for the consultation and reclaim it from the health authority. In fact the whole fee will not be reimbursed as they are expected to pay 25 per cent themselves. The proportion for other areas of the service varies according to the nature of the illness and the drugs prescribed. If a patient is hospitalised the claim will be met in full by the state apart from a small 'hotel charge'.

To ease the burden on people who have serious or long-term complaints there is a list of thirty illnesses for which total reimbursement is made. On average a patient will have to pay 25 per cent of any bill so many people take out private insurance policies to protect themselves against these payments.

This method of funding assumes that everyone can always pay the initial fee for a visit to the doctor, although vouchers are available from the local municipality for the very poor. However, social problems will inevitably be created among sections of society who find this difficult to cope with. French health care schemes are not automatic but depend on state insurance contributions. After a year of unemployment an individual no longer has an automatic right to medical care.

The other side of the picture is one of surplus. The industry has become too attractive to both investors and practitioners. Medicine has become a popular and lucrative occupation and more prescriptions are being written than ever before. France is full of high quality hospitals, far outstripping Britain and America in the ratio of beds to people. Large public wards have long since disappeared and been replaced by small pleasant rooms for two or three patients. More of these beds are empty at any one time than in comparable countries and the resulting spare capacity leads to rising costs per head.

Evidence suggests that by the year 2000 the service will be consuming 20 per cent of GNP, which has led the French government to attempt to rein back and generate extra funds, but these methods have proved unpopular.

Has Anyone Found the Solution?

All the countries we have looked at have problems with their health care systems. Rising costs and inadequate services are the main stumbling blocks which face governments. Relying on the private sector results in inequality of provision as access is limited to those who can pay. Soaring costs cause concern: the American system costs twice as much as Britain's but life expectancy is about the same. If the system is run mainly by the government it is difficult to find sufficient funds to meet all needs. A combination of the two leads to debate about the inequality of treatment in each sector, reflected in waiting lists, staffing, the availability of modern equipment and the general environment of hospitals.

The British government's aim to encourage more and more people to opt for private medicine seems initially a good idea. Not only do they pay their subscriptions to the private sector but they also continue to pay their contributions to the NHS through taxation, without using any of its services. However, it is not as simple as that. There are other costs involved.

The skilled staff used by the private sector have been trained by the public sector. They are tempted away, quite understandably, by the pleasant working environment and better pay offered in private hospitals. Many doctors divide their time between the two sectors and others are attracted to lucrative posts overseas.

In America, the state sector has had to face the problem of 'patient dumping'. These are people that private health care doesn't want to or won't treat. Even if patients are insured the company will insist that they use the public service if they are eligible. The elderly are the most significant group in this category as they are expensive to look after. Table 4.4 reflects the fact that Britain might face the same problem.

The figures suggest that the cost of private medicine for the elderly would be high, if they are acceptable at all. The other category that is often excluded is the chronically sick as insurance companies do not want to take on people who are a known risk.

The government has considered giving tax relief to encourage the development of private health care, but as there are already 5.5 million people who are insured, this would reduce revenue consider-

TABLE 4.4
The Elderly are Expensive

Age group	*Cost to the NHS per head of population*
16–64	£190
65–75	£570
75+	£1470

SOURCE: DHSS, 1988.

ably and create more problems in financing the existing system. Two-thirds of the NHS budget is spent on the elderly so if many young people opted out and were given tax relief who would pay for the old?

What Are the Alternatives?

The problems involved in providing health care for all, both cheaply and efficiently, are legion. Research is continually being carried out to develop the perfect solution, although the results would depend upon the value judgements made by those involved. In order to evaluate the alternatives we must look at some of them in greater detail.

A 'free' service

The current method of health care provision in Britain is one of the closest there is to a 'free' service. Under the current political climate it is proving to be too expensive to meet all the demands which it faces. Generally, a system which doesn't have a price will produce a level of demand which outstrips a limited supply. As demand tends to be inelastic and supply is inadequate waiting lists develop. In fact there is an ongoing debate about whether people use the service when they don't really need it, therefore increasing demand even further. Needless to say, this view receives considerable criticism but it is difficult to prove who is right.

In order to overcome the problem of excess demand several alternative systems have been developed, all of which are under scrutiny as potential alternatives to the current system.

Voluntary insurance

This is the American system. Although the growth of the UK private sector has accelerated recently only a fraction of the population is covered by insurance compared with the United States. It has been suggested that the government should attempt to increase demand for private insurance by giving tax relief on premiums (Figure 4.2),

FIGURE 4.2
The Effect of Tax Relief on the Demand for Private Health Insurance

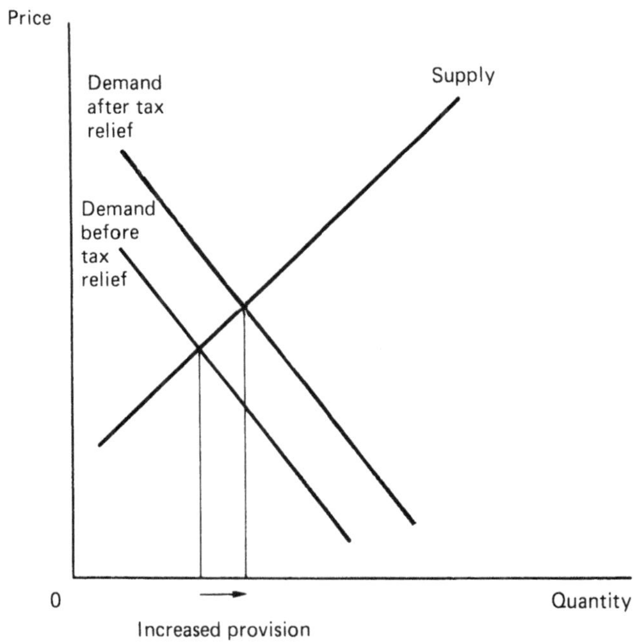

in other words, they should subsidise those who wish to opt out of the NHS and therefore put less strain on public funds.

The problem that arises from such a policy is that even if a relatively high proportion of the population take up the facility, the government still has to provide a service for all those who do not. Giving up the safety net which the NHS provides is unlikely to prove acceptable as there will always be needy groups of poor, handicapped, old and young who will have to be cared for. The other group which has to be provided for includes those who are insured but become so seriously ill that their insurance runs out.

The result would be a two-tier system needing two groups of administrators, hospitals and all the other back-up facilities that a medical service requires. This, of course, would prove to be more expensive for the economy as a whole than running one service for all and would mean that resources were being used inefficiently. The economies of scale inherent in a natural monopoly, like national health care, would be lost.

The other expense which has not been taken into account is the huge bureaucracy necessary to run a system where the majority of the population makes claims against insurance companies to pay medical bills. In America, this amounts to 20 per cent of revenue compared to the 5.5 per cent administrative costs in the NHS. Once again – is this a wise use of resources?

Compulsory insurance

This method seems to have been the European solution. Germany and France have both run their health care through a compulsory pay roll tax. The income received all goes to funding welfare services unlike Britain's national insurance contributions. Both countries have a wide choice of first-class facilities which are often privately run.

In many ways this seems to be an excellent solution as it means that everyone is contributing fairly to the provision of a good service. In effect, however, France suffers from the over-provision of facilities because the government set the prices it was prepared to pay for services too high, and now faces a situation of excess supply (Figure 4.3).

The French have chosen to reimburse people for their payments to doctors. This is also a very expensive method as 200 000 people

FIGURE 4.3
The Effect on Supply of Setting the Price Too High

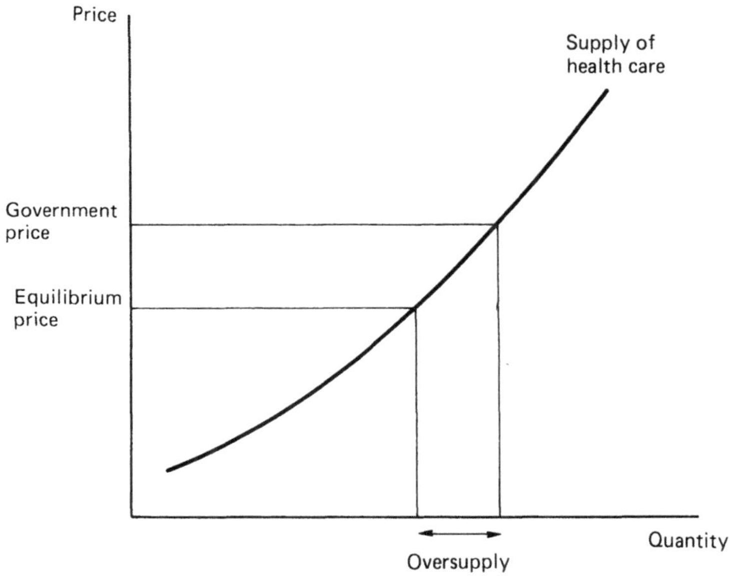

are employed to run the system. Could these people be doing something more useful? Are resources being used efficiently?

An alternative would be to allocate vouchers to each citizen on the basis of the average annual amount per head that is spent on health care – at 1988 prices this is equivalent to about £400. Individuals would then have the choice of how to use them, either for private health insurance or for treatment in the public or private sector. Initially, this would appear to be a straightforward, equitable solution which would reward efficiency by attracting more vouchers and therefore a larger share of operating and development funds. In fact it is a system fraught with difficulties.

Allocation would prove to be a problem as some people would not see a doctor all the year and therefore would not really need £400-worth of care, whereas the chronically sick might run out of funds by the end of January. If vouchers were given to everyone to spend as they wished, public money would be used to fund the private sector.

This would leave less available for the public sector, despite the fact that many of those most in need of health care would probably rely on the NHS.

A second allocative problem would arise when it came to dividing up the value of the vouchers. A patient in hospital might be cared for by doctors and nurses, X-rayed by radiographers, given treatment by physiotherapists and moved about by porters, but what are they all worth?

The voucher system would have the same effect as tax relief on the private sector. It might lead to an increase in demand as the cost to the individual would fall because the government would be subsidising premiums.

Public–private partnership

There are already many examples of the partnership between the NHS and the private sector. The shared provision and use of high-technology equipment has become common as the cost of buying such machines is prohibitive for individual hospitals.

FIGURE 4.4
Shared Resources

£1m Lithotripter

A new machine to treat kidney stones, at St Thomas's hospital London. Used by 1000 NHS and 400 private patients each year.
Made available by BUPA.

Renal Dialysis in Wales

All carried out by private companies.

Pathology tests

In some areas the private sector buys pathology tests and other services from the NHS at market prices.

Joint nurses tutor

A nurse tutor is working jointly in BUPA's Norwich hospital and the NHS hospitals in the area. Funded by BUPA.

There is scope for a great deal more development in this field as everyone benefits from sharing facilities. The examples quoted in Figure 4.4 demonstrate the relationship.

The NHS has well-established and equipped pathology labs whereas the developing private services have none. By buying in the services, the private sector saves the capital costs of setting up its own. The NHS gains because it receives revenue from selling the services and makes use of spare capacity.

The issue that does arise is whether we are really talking about 'spare capacity'. If more money was put into health care by the government would the NHS have room to provide services for the private sector? If the government's demand for health care were greater, the spare resources would be used by the public sector to reduce waiting lists. However, with constraints on spending, it is more cost effective to use facilities in this way.

The ultimate example of a link between the public and private sectors has been suggested by Tarmac, Britain's largest building firm. Tarmac wants to build its own hospital and charge the government for treating NHS patients. It would work in league with a private health care organisation to provide medical care and believes that it could save the government money.

The developments which have taken place so far in this field have been piecemeal and there has been no specific assessment of requirements and benefits. What needs to be done is a systematic investigation of the consequences for the NHS in terms of equity and efficiency.

In order to assess efficiency, NHS management must discover what revenue will be raised and what costs incurred by each proposal. The level of demand, both now and in the future, is the most significant factor in deciding what price can be charged and, therefore, how much revenue can be raised. Calculating costs is a much more difficult procedure as there are no existing systems for doing so. The government has initiated programmes to improve management and make the service more cost effective. The relevance of data collection will become more apparent as more schemes are set up to earn money for the NHS because managers will have to know the costs in detail before they make decisions. At present, this is certainly the weakest link in the buying and selling of services.

Decisions about equity will vary from one individual to another as they can only be based on value judgements. This is the fundamental issue which determines all health-care decision-making. We will look at it more fully at the end of the chapter.

Two areas of criticism have been put forward concerning the selling of services by the NHS. First, it has been suggested that it will distort future planning as there will be greater provision for high profile, income-generating areas than for more mundane needs. In other words, they will ignore social returns in favour of profit. The second complaint is that if health authorities raise money the government will simply reduce the funds it provides so there will be no rise in spending.

It is difficult to prove or disprove these ideas methodologically because we are trying to find out what would happen if . . .? This is a serious problem which often faces economists since it is impossible to have a control group as you might in physics. As a result the hypotheses remain unproven.

Health Maintenance Units

A total of 21 million Americans belong to Health Maintenance Organisations. Individuals, families or a whole workforce pay an annual fee, which is about 30 per cent lower than private insurance, to be provided with a year's health care. A group of GPs and other specialists will put together a package to meet the requirements of the group. Their aim will be to keep the clients fit, happy to sign up next year and to make themselves a profit. It has proved a very good system for keeping standards up and costs down.

An alternative organisation which would fit into the British system is the Health Maintenance Unit which has been devised by two doctors Madsen Pirie and Eamonn Butler. It would lead to the scrapping of current bureaucracy and the development of new management bodies whose funding would depend on the number of patients signing up with each group.

There are significant advantages and disadvantages to these ideas. The key advantage is that they offer more consumer choice. Opponents of the system, however, suggest that they would have to be large in order to benefit from economies of scale so there would be less choice and they would be less responsive to consumers needs. There can be little argument about the incentive they give doctors to practice preventive medicine. Keeping patients healthy reduces costs so the doctors benefit. The third advantage cited is the efficient combination of private and public resources. Nevertheless, these advantages are contradicted by the length of time they can take to set up and the higher administrative costs resulting from decentralisation. Finally, they have no mechanism to prevent underprovision.

A recent report of the parliamentary Social Services Committee suggested that they felt the disadvantages would outweigh the advantages, although there are some useful ideas for controlling doctors and organising an internal market.

Internal market

At the moment, there is a certain amount of trade taking place between health authorities but it is very fragmented and not costed on a consistent basis. The idea of an internal market would be to formalise the trade on more systematic lines and introduce competition. If a hospital has to compete for patients it is going to look much more closely at what its services are costing. Its revenue will be dependent on the numbers it attracts so that a hospital which provides good value for money will grow and develop. Inefficient ones will run short of patients and therefore decline. Increased competition should lead to greater efficiency.

FIGURE 4.5
The Effect on Costs of Economies of Scale

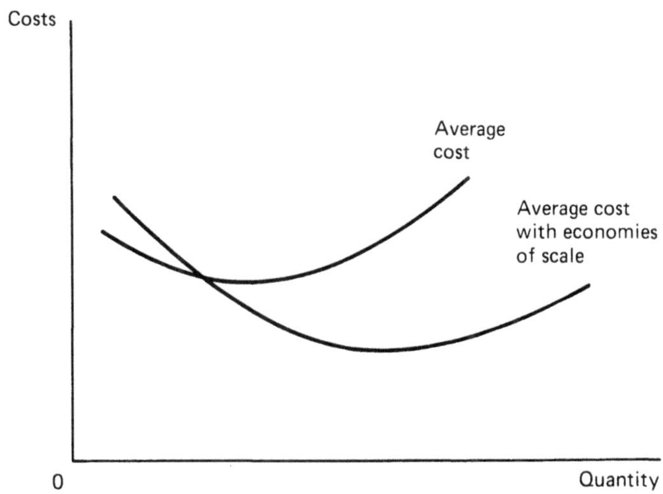

If districts choose to specialise in certain areas of medicine technological economies of scale will reduce unit costs as expensive (Figure 4.5), indivisible machinery can be used more intensively. Districts without their own equipment could buy spare capacity from other areas, perhaps at marginal cost which is below average cost.

The most serious impediment to an internal market at present are the lack of knowledge about costs within the NHS and GPs' freedom to send patients to a selected consultant. Efforts are already under way to overcome the problem of costing, but the second problem is more thorny as doctors are unwilling to give up the long-standing freedom of choice. Travel would prove to be a practical problem for patients as services might no longer be on their doorsteps. Women with children, the elderly and disabled tend to have less access to a car and therefore may not receive the treatment that they need.

It is difficult to make any judgement about the costs and benefits of an internal market at present as no experiments have been carried out. There are, currently, calls from several directions for the government do this in order to make a full evaluation before their latest plans are put into effect. They are advocating a combination of a more formally structured internal market with larger practices resembling Health Maintenance Units.

Is There a Perfect System?

We have so far investigated the problem from several points of view and none of them has proved to be without fault. A solution which may be acceptable to one individual may totally fail to meet the minimum requirements of another. Why? Because they use different yardsticks to measure acceptability, in other words, their value judgements differ.

The NHS faces a constant problem of stretching resources to meet ever greater demands. In order to cope with the necessary decision-making York University's Centre for Health Economics has developed the concept of 'quality-adjusted life-years' or QALYs. This is a cost-benefit approach to the use of resources and works in the following way.

The Heart Transplant Patient

Expected to live for ten years in perfect health

$$10 \times 1 = 10 \text{ QALYs}$$

The Leukaemia Patient

Expected to live for ten years with only half the quality of life that perfect health would give because of illness and frequent hospital trips

$$10 \times 0.5 = 5 \text{ QALYs}$$

This part of the calculation is evaluating the benefit that a patient receives. To complete the picture costs must be taken into account.

£100 000 will provide

1 heart transplant	$= 1 \times 10$	= 10 QALYs
or 5 leukemia treatments	$= 5 \times 5$	= 25 QALYs

According to these calculations, using the money to help leukaemia sufferers is a better choice because it maximises patient benefit. In fact it generates two and a half times more benefit than opting for a heart transplant.

Problem: How to allocate a budget of £14 000

GP advice to stop smoking	at £167 per QALY	= 83 QALYs
Hospital dialysis	at £14 000 per QALY	= 1 QALY

So it is much more effective to use the money to persuade people to stop smoking at the cost of not treating people in the last stage of renal failure.

The application of QALYs has raised major questions of ethics and practicality.

Ethics and Practicalities

The use of QALYs may mean that some patients are refused treatment because their quality of life will not justify the costs incurred. This sounds very unjust but it needs to be looked at in the context of scarce resources. At the beginning of the chapter we observed that it would be possible to spend the entire GNP on health care. Obviously this is not possible so choices have to be made, whatever the level of funding. Perhaps it is more unethical to use the random decision-making that has been the more usual technique, as this will result in using scarce resources inefficiently.

If health care is being provided for those who will benefit most, social implications may arise. Professor Alan Maynard, the Director of the Centre for Health Economics at York, suggests that in order to overcome the problems of some groups benefiting more than others, the government would have to institute radical policies in the fields of income, wealth and education.

There is considerable criticism of current attempts at measurement but the QALYs technique is still in its infancy and research is continuing to refine it.

However, the development of new medical treatments is usually expensive and if everything had to be cost effective it might be impossible. To overcome this problem a research budget would have to be kept separate from general hospital funding.

The introduction of such a system would alter the behaviour of hospital management, the medical supplies industry and politicians, since they would all have to justify their actions in terms of costs and benefits.

The debate over the acceptability of QALYs returns us to the topic of equity and value judgements. For some people, the choices being advocated here are anathema and the ideas for the introduction of the market into the NHS are equally abhorrent. The NHS was established on the assumption of free access and rationing took place on the basis of doctors' decisions, waiting lists and the budget for the district. Anyone who puts free access at the top of their list of value judgements is unlikely to accept the idea of selling medical care.

The solutions which are coming under the closest scrutiny at the moment involve the market mechanism. Both internal markets and joint ventures with the private sector require a much greater knowledge of costs and a more efficient use of resources. Selling services should increase the budget for the NHS and can be looked upon as a trade-off because cross-subsidisation will provide better care within the system. However, the point at which the trade-off is acceptable will depend on an individual's value judgements.

The answer to the question 'Is there a perfect system?' is obviously 'No!' All we can attempt to do is to optimise efficiency and balance it with equity.

5 Conservation and the Environment

Are Economic Growth and Conservation Compatible?

Ever since man ceased being hunters and gatherers and started farming we have used the environment we live in for our own benefit. As the country industrialised the pressure on the landscape increased. We dammed streams for water power, we left heaps of spoil from our mines and wondered what to do with radioactive waste. For a long time, industry was unregulated but as people became aware of the damage that was being done we started to pass laws in an attempt to control this deterioration of our towns, cities and countryside. In 1650, long before the Industrial Revolution, laws were passed which banned the use of coal fires in London. But laws about pollution are difficult to police and enforce and often the fines which are imposed on firms that break them are minimal.

Why Do Firms not Comply with the Law?

If these firms installed the necessary equipment and staff to ensure that their effluent always met the standards laid down in law, their costs would rise. The fines which are imposed are not a sufficient deterrent and therefore do not provide an incentive for firms to clean up their production processes. As we discussed in the opening chapter, private costs are currently low as they do not include the costs that would be incurred in preventing pollution.

BIG BUSINESSES FLOUT LAWS TO POLLUTE RIVERS

Many of Britain's largest firms are ignoring environmental controls and regularly dumping illegal levels of pollution into rivers without fear of prosecution.

A list of firms which reads like a Who's Who of British industry are habitually breaking laws which are designed to protect the environment against contamination of water and the destruction of fish and wildlife.

Yet the water authorities, which are among the country's worst offenders, with effluent discharges from their sewage works, have proved strangely reluctant to prosecute the big companies.

Last year the number of reported cases in England and Wales rose to a record 23,253 with 1,402 of the incidents regarded as serious.

But there were only 288 prosecutions and many of the companies found guilty received conditional discharges or fines as low as a few hundred pounds. In one recent court case a Humberside chemical company received a conditional discharge for a spillage which dyed the River Hull blue.

The rivers of the north and Midlands face the worst threat of industrial pollution but the southern rivers face increasing agricultural pollution which can often be more toxic than the by-products of industry.

The hazards were highlighted by police inspector Malcolm Beavers who waded into the River Aire to pull out a drowning man. Within days he fell ill and lost his physical strength, memory and concentration. This was diagnosed as post-viral fatigue syndrome, a condition which can result from contact with water contaminated with bacteria from sewage works.

When asked why there are so few prosecutions, a spokeswoman for the Water Authorities Association said 'It is very high in manpower costs to prosecute and when you do get the firms to court, the fines are abysmally low.'

Adapted from *The Sunday Times*, 13 November 1988

In many other ways, economic growth has damaged our environment but, as usual, there are two sides to the argument. If there had been no economic growth what sort of a country would Britain be today? Could we still exist in a developed world as an agrarian, village dwelling economy? Obviously not. As the free market encourages negative externalities, methods of controlling them must be introduced if we are going to have the benefits of growth without damaging the environment.

Everyone expects to be able to drive their cars and have endless supplies of pure water from their taps, but equally they expect to walk in the countryside and enjoy the wilder parts of Britain. People are horrified when droughts mean that they cannot water the garden or wash the car but they are unwilling to make the sacrifice required to maintain the water supply. Everyone would like the reservoir, motorway or railway line to be built somewhere else. The 'Not in My Back Yard' or NIMBY syndrome is very understandable, no one wants their own environment harmed. The solution is to turn to cost–benefit analysis to make the evaluation.

Water

In 1976 and 1984, south-west England was faced with drought conditions which drained reservoirs dry and led to a public outcry. The region depends on tourism for its livelihood and demand falls rapidly if people think there will not be enough water for a bath or for St Austell brewery to make any beer! The solution was to build new reservoirs so that the crisis would never occur again. Everyone agreed that this was necessary but they failed to agree when it came to choosing a site.

Each suggestion carries an opportunity cost. The national parks were considered as protected land but a site was finally chosen at Roadford which would solve the problems for Plymouth, part of south-west Devon and north Devon. The decision was taken in 1975, after the first drought, but it took until 1985, after the second drought, for them to be given the go-ahead. Why?

The benefits of the new reservoir were obvious. Plenty of water would mean the tourist industry could develop further and prevent the traumas involved in shortages. There would also be water sports, fishing and bird watching as additional benefits from the reservoir. The costs, however, were more complex. The water authority was faced with opposition from local residents, the District Councils and the National Farmers Union who all faced different 'costs' if the reservoir were built.

The local residents' costs resulted from the loss of their homes as the waters rose. A money value can be calculated for the house that is lost and the cost of finding a new one, but what is hard to evaluate is the disruption of life that is caused by the move. The district councils saw a very different future ahead when the reservoir was built. Their area would change from a quiet rural retreat, just off the tourist route, to a recreational centre for people from miles around. This would require the provision of facilities to cope with the influx. The farmers' costs were perhaps the most serious as they were threatened with losing their source of income when their land was flooded.

All these cases were presented to the public enquiry. The decision went in favour of the water authority because the benefits outweighed the costs. In other words, the social benefits were more significant than the private costs.

Environmental pressures encouraged the water authority to incorporate into their costings schemes to protect the wild life of the area. This involved investigations to monitor the effect of the new flows of water on salmon and trout as the dam would cut off nursery areas. The area was cleared at times which would cause the least interference with the life cycle of animals which lived there, and plants of ecological importance were moved to appropriate locations above the top water level. Parts of the reservoir are designated to become nature reserves.

Archaeologists were involved in work on sites which would be below water level. They looked at the medieval origins of some of the farmsteads and searched for links with prehistoric times.

Green Belt

NORTHERN GREEN BELT IN DANGER

Large tracts of countryside in England's north and Midlands are coming under intense pressure from developers looking for alternatives to the overcrowded southeast.

Local authorities, faced with a building boom on the edge of some of Britain's most run-down industrial areas, are increasingly willing to consider sacrificing green belt land in return for jobs and investment.

Planners in Rotherham, Chester, Birmingham, Solihull and Coventry have all earmarked areas of green belt which they hope to open up to prestige companies.

But the building boom has brought a warning from the Council for the Protection of Rural England. They say that the government and local authorities are not doing enough to force developers to build on derelict industrial land in the north. 'It is important to guard against the idea that the countryside in the southeast is any more special than that in the north.'

The increasing pressure on land in areas that have been depressed for many years has placed local authorities in an awkward position. Many have been unable to attract private investment on the derelict land and say they cannot afford to develop it themselves.

Rotherham which is planning to release 400 acres of green belt land along the M1 and M18 corridors, has witnessed its traditional industries decline but says it does not have the money to reclaim the urban dereliction left behind.

The council insists that it has a good record on protecting the environment. But it is under fire for granting planning permission for three new hotels on green belt land.

Adapted from *The Sunday Times*, 20th November 1988.

The councillors of Rotherham and similar towns have found themselves on the horns of a dilemma. The have to decide whether to sacrifice the environment for economic growth which they desperately need. The current trend in industrial building is the hi-tech business park on a green field site. The hotels being built near Rotherham would not be attracted to the area if they were confined to sites of inner city dereliction.

They seem to be taking the view that the benefits which the new developments bring to the town in the form of jobs, more income and therefore more spending power, will outweigh the costs incurred in losing some countryside. Perhaps as these towns grow wealthier and the new industry develops they will be able to clear these inner city sites.

Is it worth it?

Could we cut social costs by going for 'zero growth'? This idea means that we should have none of the growth which adds to pollution and spoils the environment. This is a very crude technique as it simply stops all growth, whether there are social costs involved or not. A more efficient way of dealing with the external effects of growth is to tackle the problems directly as the zero growth solution merely distorts the market.

Government policy should attempt to regulate pollution and damage to the environment in order to achieve a position where the marginal benefit from producing more goods is equal to the marginal costs of pollution to society. In other words, where marginal social costs and marginal social benefits are equal. This could be done by taxes on pollution and controls on development to ensure that increasing output stays within these guidelines.

In trying to put this into practice, serious problems arise in putting a monetary value on the costs. Cleaning up a river can be calculated in terms of the resources that are used to do it, but how do you evaluate the countryside which is lost outside Rotherham? It is difficult to assess these situations objectively because everyone is influenced by value judgements.

At present, governments tend to be assessed on how rapidly the economy is expanding. The measurement of Gross National Product is very simplistic as it takes no account of the externalities, whether costs or benefits, incurred in this growth of output. If such measurements could incorporate a quality of life index so that the costs and benefits of growth could be more accurately compared, governments might be less willing to sacrifice the environment for the sake of a higher place in the league table. Again, however, decisions are fraught with problems because value judgements inevitably underlie any 'desirable' level of growth.

Environmental Issues

Environmental problems vary in nature. Some originate from changes in our lifestyle and will continue unless measures are taken to control the cause. Others are the result of a one-off development which usually has a direct effect on a relatively small area. The same theories can be used to analyse each problem.

The decision as to what must be done is made easier by weighing up the costs and benefits. This is obviously easier on a small scale but even then we are faced with the problem of differing value judgements. Someone will always be dissatisfied.

The more general problems, like acid rain, are more difficult to evaluate until the damage becomes so evident that there is a consensus of opinion that something must be done.

Acid Rain: A Continuing Problem

The problem

Forests and lakes in north-west Europe have been dying steadily over the last few decades. Tests on the lakes have shown that the level of acidity has risen to a point where they can no longer support fish. Loch Fleet in Scotland has been used as the base for a research project run by the coal and electricity industry. The graph shows the decline in the number of brown trout caught in the loch since the 1930s (Figure 5.1).

FIGURE 5.1
The Decline of Trout in Loch Fleet

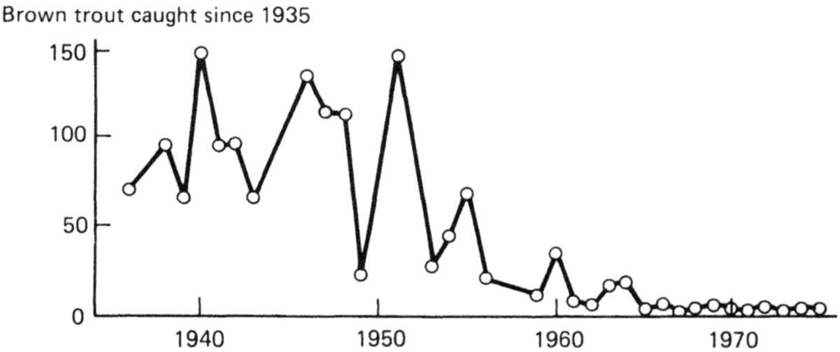

SOURCE: CEGB, *New Life for Acid Waters: The Loch Fleet Project*, 1987.

Studies show that the loch became rapidly more acidic from 1970 and when the project was started in 1984 there were no fish to be found in either the loch or its tributaries as the water conditions were not fit for them.

It is not only the natural environment that is in danger but the stonework of our historic buildings is also being threatened by an invisible agent.

The cause

Acid rain is a term that is used to describe both pollution in the air and contaminated rain. When coal is burnt in power stations sulphur dioxide and nitrogen oxide are emitted from the chimneys. These are converted into dilute sulphuric and nitric acids when they react with other chemicals in the air. They are also produced by the reaction of sunlight on emissions from car exhausts and industry. This mixture can then be carried in the atmosphere and deposited hundreds of miles away.

Britain has been blamed for a great many of the problems that have occurred in Germany and Scandinavia, although research has shown that sulphur dioxide could come from North America and Russia as well as mainland Europe itself.

Since the Industrial Revolution industry has been polluting the atmosphere with both these gases. It is only the recent realisation of the effects which have led attitudes to change. Figure 5.2 shows the rise in sulphur dioxide emissions and how it will diminish in future.

FIGURE 5.2
Sulphur Dioxide Emissions in the UK: Past and Future

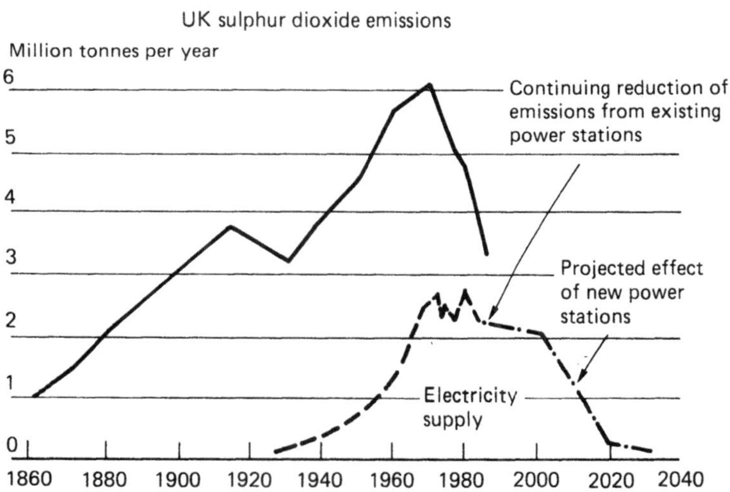

SOURCE: CEGB, *New Life for Acid Waters*, 1987.

Before the electricity industry spent millions on reducing these emissions, they wanted to be sure that this really was the cause of the dying lakes and forests.

There were several areas that needed to be researched because some lakes with lower acid levels were fishless while others maintained a stock despite greater acidity. As most water reaches lakes through the soil around them, the soil needed investigating.

The cure

Having decided that power station emissions were contributing to the acidity of rainfall, the electricity industry set about looking for solutions. There were two different problems that had to be resolved. First, how to repair the environmental damage that had already been done by bringing back life to the dying lakes, and secondly, how to prevent any further damage by reducing the output of harmful gases.

This work was essential because a great deal of money was at stake. We are already aware of the costs involved in allowing acid rain to continue as the situation would simply get worse. If the adaptations were not carefully considered, the costs of curing the problems would be higher than necessary and the cost of electricity would rise as a result.

The sum of £1.5 million was spent on the project at Loch Fleet where experiments were carried out to find the most effective technique for spreading lime on the adjacent land to reduce the acidity of both soil and water. Within a month trout could survive at the outflow of the loch.

The second challenge, to remove the harmful gases from the emissions, has two possible solutions. Both have the advantage of producing by-products which can be sold and therefore reduce the cost. They are nevertheless still very expensive so the electricity industry is investigating the possibility of removing the sulphur from the coal before it is burnt. Different systems have to be installed to remove the nitrogen oxides.

Taxation and legislation can both be used to prevent firms or individuals polluting the environment. Tax is only a solution if the perpetrators can be identified, which is often impossible. Anti-pollution laws are often the solution as they apply to everyone – a technique now being used to remove harmful emissions from car exhausts. All new cars must be able to run on lead-free petrol because the law states that catalytic convertors must be installed.

The costs and benefits

If nothing were done, the cost to the environment would be very great as more and more forests and lakes would suffer as acid levels in the soils rose. But both homes and industry would benefit as electricity prices would not have to rise to pay the costs of producing less noxious gases. The long-run consequences, if no action were taken, would be increasingly serious and as a spokesman for Friends of the Earth put it, 'Something's just got to be done.'

The costs of the clean up

● Fitting 'flue gas desulphurisation' system to some existing power stations	£2 billion
additional costs:	
• lost output during conversion	?
• cost at other power stations	?
• extra cost at new stations	15%
• reduction in efficiency	10%
• running costs once installed	£110 million per year
resulting income:	
— sales of by-product: gypsum	Initially small, later a liability
● Fitting 'low NO_x burners'	£200 million
● The Loch Fleet project	£1.5 million (including research costs)

This gives a broad idea of the scale of the costs involved in curing this acid rain. Many of the figures are estimates others are simply not available.

The benefits

Putting a figure on past and future damage is impossible but the benefits from controlling emissions now are that we can restore our forests and lakes to their former state. The timber and fishing industries will gain from the work and the environment will be protected from the destructive effects of a growing European economy.

The Channel Tunnel: The Impact of a New Development

Some People Look at the Costs

'A heated meeting of 500 villagers, worried about the high speed rail link to the tunnel, was told it would be unlikely there would be money for expensive environmental protection measures.'

'In the village along the road from me, the route will go through the primary school where both my children learnt their alphabet. If this route is chosen it will have to close.'

'Private capital is interested in private gain, getting the highest amount of money it can for the least amount expended, and that is no bad thing. But is it appropriate in the case of the Channel Tunnel railway? How do you square those commercial principles with spending money to mitigate the misery and ugliness this project may imposê on people living nearby?'

'The Kent Impact Study was a business promotion to exploit the Channel Tunnel. Is it right to drag down to Kent every bit of industry they can?'

'Being designated "the county growth point" meant that Ashford would become the dustbin for everything the rest of the country doesn't want.'

Observations of people who fear the environmental implications of the Channel Tunnel on the Kent countryside.

Others Look at the Benefit

'The Channel Tunnel will shorten journey times between London and other European Community capitals. Times to Paris, Brussels and Amsterdam will be almost halved. Dinner at the Tour d'Argent?'

'I see many British chaps in suits carrying brief cases,' said Her Majesty's Honorary Consul in Boulogne. 'They are definitely not day trippers; they're sniffing the market.'

'Kent businessmen were apathetic. They argued: "The tunnel is never going to be built; even if it is it won't concern me." Now there is a manifestly different enthusiasm.'

'Kent County Council has set up a special unit to exploit 1992 and the tunnel. The council leader sees Kent and the Nord Pas de Calais as a common region with the Channel a unifying attraction rather than a barrier. The two sides have made a joint application to Brussels for funding, and together they are seeking overseas investment and exploring ways of exploiting tourism.'

'The tunnel is a catalyst. If we play our cards right we can get considerable growth from it.'

Observations by those who are looking for the advantages the tunnel might bring.

The environmental factors involved in the Channel Tunnel are the main source of concern to the people of Kent. It is not the only area of anxiety; Dover fears that it will face unemployment problems because the demand for the ferries will decline once the tunnel opens. The depressed regions of Britain also have their doubts as they wonder why such large-scale investment should be concentrated in the South East.

The greatest direct impact on the environment comes from the high-speed rail track which has to be built if the tunnel is to become an integral part of the European railway network. The route that is selected finally will inevitably mean the destruction of businesses, communities, homes and gardens, as well as conservation areas. All those who are affected are suffering from planning blight and cannot sell their homes at a price that they are prepared to accept. Compensation will be paid to those whose properties are pulled down but many will find that their lives are changed from rural tranquillity by the proximity of the line. The county council are looking on the positive side. If the track is built it will encourage freight to pass straight through Kent and therefore lessen congestion on the roads. They are also hoping that high-speed commuter trains will be able to use the lines and therefore improve travel for those who live in Kent and work in London.

The site of the tunnel entrance and terminal takes 350 acres of countryside and will inevitably change the environment dramatically. Efforts have been made to confine the impact on neighbouring villages, to avoid sensitive areas of nature conservation and to conceal the tunnel works when it is complete. Parliament has granted Kent unique controls over landscaping and vehicle access in order to ensure an acceptable result.

The indirect factors which affect Kent result from the attraction of industry and warehouses to this major new link with Europe. Many people fear that planning consent will be freely granted to these newcomers as economic growth will be the main concern. Ashford, for example, has been a designated growth point for twenty years and it has made little difference, but now the town's publicity material talks of 'challenge' and 'destiny', so the future looks very different.

Kent County Council's ambition is to get the best it can from the tunnel without wrecking the Garden of England. Their aim is economic growth and they realise that there will be some effect on the environment but they also appreciate that the Kent countryside is of economic value in its own right. Its rural character is a great draw for people who want to set up businesses and destroying this would be to kill the goose that lays the golden egg. They claim that what is proposed is relatively small but because the tunnel has been headline news, developments have been exaggerated. Not everyone agrees.

Is it worth it?

Estimates suggest that cross Channel travel will have doubled by the end of the century. The Eurotunnel consortium envisages absorbing a considerable proportion of this growth. Figure 5.3 shows current and future demand for Channel crossings. It suggests that the tunnel

FIGURE 5.3
The Cross Channel Market: A Changing Pattern

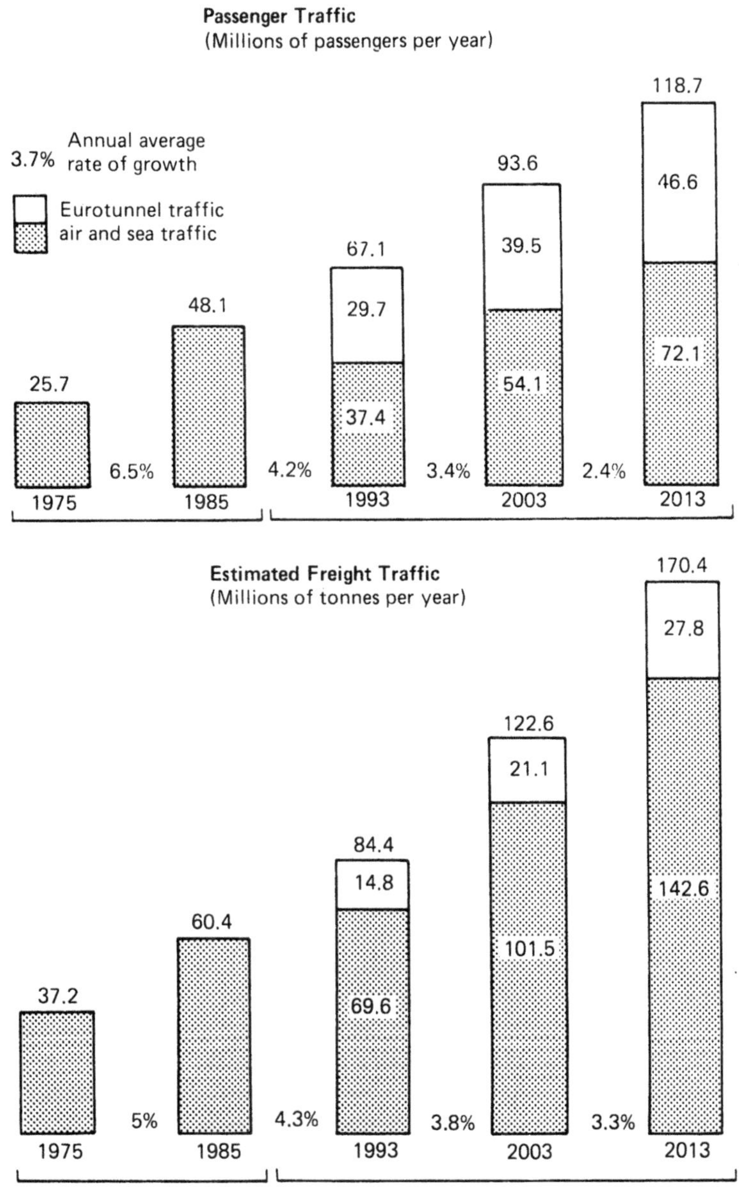

SOURCE: Eurotunnel Information, Paris, November 1987.

will mop up the element of growth rather than affect the existing services, apart from passengers where the ferries will not regain their existing position until the turn of the century.

The Direct Benefits

- London to Paris in 2h 35mins
- Speedy delivery for goods to all parts of Europe
- No delays from stormy seas
- Round the clock service
- Tickets, customs and passport control in 15 minutes

The Indirect Benefits

- 5000 new jobs during construction
- Increased demand for materials and equipment for construction
- More jobs in the tunnel's hinterland

Starts on a tunnel have been made in the past but this time it is going to be completed. The argument, therefore, has to be based on how to gain the most benefit for the lowest cost to society as a whole. In making decisions on future developments, the planners' concern is maintaining a balance. The Kent Impact Study makes this clear when it says: 'Obviously, any degree of additional development will have some environmental effects which must be weighed against the value put on jobs created.'

This 'value' will be given a different weighting by different people. The family who will lose their home and the business man who sees his firm growing will have disparate views on the subject. It is impossible to escape from the fact that whatever the decision, it is a value judgement. Planners in the area use their skills to try to produce a solution which minimises the negative effects and maximises the positive effects.

The decision

Both examples have demonstrated the use of costs and benefits in deciding whether to go ahead with a proposal or project. In each case the answer was, to some extent, a foregone conclusion. A rail track will be built . . . but where? Acid rain must be controlled . . . but to what level?

As long as the marginal social benefit is greater than the marginal social cost the project is viable. By equating *MSC* and *MSB* the net gain to the environment is equivalent to the cost of its cure. Air pollution could be cut out completely but the cost would be so great that it would outweigh the benefits, and we would have to give up many other things to pay for it. The price of electricity, for example, would have to be much higher so the price of many other goods would rise as a result. It seems simple to work this out and decide the 'acceptable' level of pollution, but again we are faced with alternative views which influence people's attitudes.

Cost–benefit analysis tries to give market values to all aspects of the project but hits trouble in the very same way. How do you put a value on the loss of a historic building, a beautiful stretch of countryside or the village pub? When looking for a site for the third London airport, the Roskill Commission simply gave up their attempt to do this and confined themselves to things that could be measured, despite the fact that these were the main focus of debate in the areas concerned.

Do We Make the 'Right' Decisions?

People often wonder why there is a preservation order on the local Gaumont cinema or Battersea Power Station. They regard them as hideous and definitely not worth preserving. Wouldn't it be better to pull it down and build a nice new leisure centre or even an office block? Equally, when the local cinema is threatened with destruction people organise petitions to prevent it. Who is right?

We look back at 'acts of vandalism' in the past, when buildings which we regard as beautiful have been destroyed. At the time they were thought to be old fashioned, ugly and much better replaced by something contemporary. Will people look back on the twentieth century in the same way?

Obviously, we simply cannot preserve everything as the country would become fossilised and we could only sell ourselves to the world as a museum. Somehow we have to find the balance between conservation and development. There are some clear boundaries. We are not going to pull down the Tower of London or build a motorway through the heart of the Lake District but there are pressures on many other aspects of our environment. The role of the planners is very significant as they have to look at schemes objectively and weigh up the relative costs and benefits involved, using the tools of the economist tempered with an awareness of the local environment.

6 The Inner Cities

The Cities in Riot

In the early 1980s urban unrest struck several of our major cities. London, Liverpool and Bristol all suffered outbreaks of violence resulting from the economic and social decline in their inner city areas.

Two centuries earlier, the Industrial Revolution had brought great changes to many people's lives as the attraction of work had drawn them from a rural life in the village to the growing cities. Narrow streets of houses were built to accommodate this influx and the newcomers congregated in such areas. The cities grew rich on coal, steel and cotton and continued to expand.

As time passed, the more affluent moved to the leafier suburbs, a trend which was reinforced in the 1950s by the development of new towns. In general, the people who moved away were the young and go-ahead who thought that their families would have a better life away from the grimy city.

Throughout history poor areas of inner cities have attracted immigrants and refugees. The Huguenots, for example, who fled from France in the seventeenth century took up residence in Spitalfields, an area of London which has continued to be the home of newcomers. As they usually have little money they are looking for cheap accommodation. As these trends continued some districts became populated by the old, the poor and immigrants.

These movements of population were exacerbated by our changing industrial structure. The decline of heavy industry led to unemployment in the cities. Sheffield, for example, lost 40 000 jobs in steel alone in the 1970s and 1980s. By 1988, 14 per cent of the adult workforce were unemployed. Youth unemployment reached 90 per cent in Hyde Park, one of the city's central districts. What incentive is there for school leavers in such a situation? Doing well has little effect as there are simply no jobs to go to, so truancy rises and achievement falls.

As firms closed down there was little encouragement for new industries to develop. Who would want to start up a firm in the midst of industrial decline and dereliction? The more jobs that were lost, the greater was the effect on the area because if jobs go, incomes go. People then have little money to spend so the shops and other services close down and even more jobs are lost. The multiplier effect works downwards to exaggerate the initial loss. It is the start of a gloomy spiral which is very hard to end.

As things get worse the social costs become apparent. As unemployment rises more and more people fall below the threshold for local taxation, so each authority has less to spend on services such as education and housing. The result is that those who are most in need suffer the worst provision unless the government steps in to help them out. With poor housing and little incentive to make the most of education the future looks bleak.

The costs can also be measured in terms of the resources that are being wasted. Land in many of our major industrial cities is standing vacant because the cost of clearing it is too great for the local authority to bear alone. Birmingham, for example, has 2000 acres of derelict land, a daunting challenge for any city.

The unemployed labour force is a second wasted resource. Not only is it costing the country large sums in benefits but we are also losing the goods and services that could be produced.

What Can Be Done?

DEVELOPERS BRING NEW LIFE TO BLIGHTED LANDSCAPE

The view from the first floor offices of the Sheffield Development Corporation is the best reminder of what its work is all about.

A mile from the M1 motorway the staff look out over acres of derelict land, once the home of a thriving steel concern. The people who live in the few pockets of housing which remain have got used to gazing out on nothing. But the Development Corporation, with £50m of Environment Department money to spend on reviving 2,000 acres of the Lower Don Valley, plans to change all that.

Initially it was opposed by the city council which saw it as a threat to local control. But the hatchet was quickly buried. As proof of its commitment to local interests, the corporation is the only one of its kind to appoint a community director.

Hugh Sykes, the chairman says: 'There are 20m people within a two hour drive. We are superbly located and for businesses thinking of a move, we have a lot going for us.'

His aim is to improve the environment, encourage existing businesses and attract new ones. The corporation hopes to persuade national companies to use Sheffield as their training centre. 'We are in an excellent place geographically and we can offer the facilities of the university and polytechnic and soon access to almost every variety of sporting arena.'

Already the scaffolding is in place for the £230m Meadowhall regional shopping and leisure centre, alongside the motorway, which is expected to be completed in two years.

Equally high on the corporation's list is a much smaller building: the viewing platform which is to be erected at Wincobank, giving a panoramic impression of the Don Valley desolation, and the scale of the regeneration task.

Adapted from *The Sunday Times*, 13 November 1988

The people of Sheffield have learnt that cooperation is needed to overcome problems on this scale. Councillors, industry, trade unions, community groups and the development corporation now work in partnership.

The steel industry has virtually disappeared and the city is looking to the future. They are trying to attract high technology firms and are developing a science park, a cultural industries quarter and the regional shopping centre mentioned in the article. Winning the bid for the 1991 World Student Games has raised Sheffield's esteem. They are building facilities for swimming, diving, cycling, athletics and a range of other sporting activities. In future, they are expecting to be able to host national and international sporting events which will all bring money and jobs to the city.

Construction jobs are already being created and the aim is to ensure that as many local people as possible are employed. An agreement has already been made with the construction companies to recruit from the city, to ensure the inclusion of ethnic minorities and to be prepared to train people who do not have the right skills. The city council wants to guarantee that the local residents benefit as much as possible from these developments.

Task force to the rescue?

The Confederation of British Industry has come to the conclusion that industry must take more responsibility for the economic and social well-being of the surrounding regions. Allowing decline to spiral out of control affects both employees and customers.

Newcastle on Tyne has been selected for the initial programme. The scheme is to develop 'flagship' projects which will be a focus for further investment. In Newcastle, the old Opera House has been revived as the Tyne Theatre and is a centrepiece for the renovation of the West End as an 'arts village'. There have also been improvements on some of the town's housing estates and an advertising campaign to attract people and industry to the area.

The CBI's aim is to produce a package which is easily transferable to other cities in need of help. The experience that they have acquired in Newcastle will help them to develop 'template' policies for use elsewhere. If it is to work, the task force chairman realises that businessmen must accept four basic ideas. First, the leadership must come from industry. Secondly, it can be done, industry has developed the strategies. Thirdly, charity alone is inadequate. Investment must be viable if it is to create new wealth. Lastly, industry must be prepared to give up time, resources and personnel.

The CBI seeks to coordinate many different organisations which have been involved in inner city regeneration, using private sector returns as a catalyst for further wealth generation.

Compacts

Compacts are an idea culled from the United States. By closer liaison between schools and industry, they are intended to improve school leavers' chances of employment. In inner city areas there is often a mismatch between the qualifications of this age group and the skills industry requires.

The scheme is based on firms giving priority in employment and relevant training to fifth-year school leavers in schools with which they have made a compact. The students must have attained certain agreed goals, both personal and academic, which show that they would make successful employees.

The East London Compact, which was the first in Britain, initially involved 500 students, 300 jobs and 40 local companies, rapidly expanded to include 100 firms and 10 schools. The idea has since spread to much of the rest of London and the government has provided £12 million to develop the scheme in cities throughout the country.

Why did firms join the scheme? Many had been recruiting among local school leavers with insufficient skills of literacy and numeracy. Applicants expected to be given 'interesting' work straight away or suspected that they were being exploited. Others did not have sufficient social skills to dress appropriately for an interview. These problems led to firms employing commuters into the inner cities instead of local residents.

The main benefit of compacts is to alleviate this waste of resources. With the sort of encouragement and objectives that the students are given, they can help themselves to become more employable. This means that the earning capacity of the area rises and the multiplier effect gets to work and generates more wealth. School governors have backed the scheme because it gives young people, their families and the community the chance of a better future.

Industry will benefit from being involved in compacts because of the changing demographic structure. As the number of school leavers declines rapidly in the next few years, firms are going to be competing to recruit staff. A firm that is involved in the scheme will have developed close links with schools and therefore will be able to overcome the problems more easily.

Compacts provide both private and external benefits at comparatively little cost. The firms and the students involved gain from the links and as employment rises in the local area the whole economic and social environment improves.

Government assistance

The main thrust of the government's policy on the inner cities has been to involve private sector finance. Industry has tended to avoid these areas as Sheffield has demonstrated because they have little attraction for new and vigorous firms.

In the early 1980s Enterprise Zones were set up where taxes and planning regulations were relaxed to encourage investment. This has resulted in the establishment of new firms and the growth of jobs. There have been some costs but we will investigate them further when looking at Docklands.

Since then there has been a succession of schemes which has been designed to clear derelict land and give grants to new firms and developers. In 1988, these were remodelled as the Urban Programme, which gives grants to specific projects in fifty-seven areas of greatest need, and the City Grant, which is paid direct to developers in order to minimise bureaucracy.

Much of the work is aimed at helping small businesses to succeed. Enterprise Allowances help unemployed people to start their own businesses by giving them £40 a week for the first year, managed workshops provide small premises with secretarial, catering and advisory services on the site, and the Small Firms Service gives information and counselling to help firms become viable and profitable. The same sort of help is available from local enterprise agencies which are backed by industry through the provision of funds, advice and personnel.

The need to coordinate the work of the public and private sector has led to the establishment of City Action Teams and Task Forces. The work in Sheffield demonstrated the fact that change happens more rapidly and effectively when there is an overall plan which incorporates everyone's efforts.

The most far-reaching change has been the establishment of Urban Development Corporations. These have the power to acquire, reclaim and service land and put buildings to effective use. They have planning powers over the areas for which they are responsible and this has given rise to criticisms from local politicians who feel that their powers have been usurped and the interests of local people are not being taken into account. This, again, is a theme which will be further developed in the section on docklands.

London and Merseyside were the first two UDCs to be set up and a further six, including Sheffield, have since been added.

The London Docklands: A Large-scale Development

The docklands area of London had been in decline since the docks started falling into disuse. As ships increased in size and containerisation grew in importance in the 1960s and 1970s, the Victorian docks became obsolete. This led to unemployment as the population of the area had traditionally been involved in dock related industries. The local councils had declining resources as the income level of the area fell so housing and other social services suffered.

Industrial development around London was happening on green field sites down the Thames Valley to the west and around towns like Crawley, which had the growth point of Gatwick Airport close at hand. Docklands faced the problems of the declining regions in other parts of the country, no one wanted to invest in an area that appeared derelict and would be expensive to clear before work could begin. Something had to be done on a large scale if regeneration were to begin.

The London Docklands Development Corporation (LDDC) was set up by the government in July 1981. Before it was allowed to go ahead there was an investigation by an all party select committee because of the number of objections to the proposal. The concerns expressed by the pressure groups centred on the effects the development would have on the locality. They feared that control was being taken out of their hands as local democracy would be reduced. They feared that new housing would be mainly for the affluent, not the locals, whose living conditions were inadequate. They feared that new jobs would be for outsiders. They feared that the best sites would go to outsiders. Many of the planning functions of the LDDC seemed to duplicate the local councils' so resources would be wasted.

After looking at the developments that have taken place we will see if these fears were justified.

The New Docklands

The LDDC describes the changes that are taking place as the creation of the 'Metropolitan Water City of the twenty-first century'. An area of 22 square kilometres around the old docks is being developed to create businesses, houses and jobs.

Its remit was described by Reg Ward, the first Chief Executive as follows: 'to bring land and buildings into effective use, stimulate existing and new industry and commerce, create an attractive environment and ensure the right housing and social facilities were created to encourage people to live and work in the area'.

By 1988, £4400 million of private investment had been attracted to the scheme on top of £441 million of public money. This has been used for the 15 000 new homes, the 100 million square metres of commercial and industrial development and the necessary infrastructure to support them.

Docklands had always faced the problem of poor communications with the rest of London so a new network was essential if the plans were to work. The Docklands Light Railway provides a link with the City and the airport has connections with Paris and Brussels. Within the area a new system of roads has had to be built to service both homes and industry.

Firms moving into the area have brought 20 000 new jobs with them, although some of these have been the relocation of existing jobs. There has been a skills mismatch as local people do not often have the necessary skills to be employed. In order to overcome this problem Skillnet has been set up in liaison with the local authorities. The necessary finance has come from government agencies and the EEC Social Fund. It provides training courses in the type of jobs that are becoming available in Docklands and responds particularly to employers' recruitment needs. Compacts are also helping to develop the appropriate skills of local school leavers.

The LDDC will provide advice for firms which want to set up in the area through its Business Centre. It helps firms to apply for government grants which are available to inner urban areas. The Isle of Dogs, a part of Docklands, is also eligible for extra assistance as it is an Enterprise Zone.

The Times and the *Daily Telegraph* have built new printing works, several firms have moved into new headquarters offices, there is a television studios complex and a wine bottling plant. Several groups of smaller units have been built to accommodate new firms. Altogether over 600 new firms had entered Docklands by 1989. There is a tendency for the industry to be hi-tech so there has been a demand for skilled labour which Skillnet is helping to meet.

The economic success of the scheme is undeniable because regeneration has certainly taken place. The problems which have arisen are the result of the social impact on the local population.

The anxieties mentioned at the beginning of this section have been justified in varying degrees.

Unemployment

The LDDC was established on land in three London boroughs – Tower Hamlets, Southwark and Newham. By 1981, all the docks had closed and the resulting effect on employment was very severe. It was discovered that for every job that was lost in the port industries three other jobs in allied trades disappeared. By 1981, male unemployment in Docklands stood at 21.4 per cent. Table 6.1 covers an area larger than the LDDC but gives some idea of the problems that they faced.

The high number of unskilled workers and low number of professional workers meant that it was difficult to bring in the type of job that could easily be filled by the local unemployed.

TABLE 6.1
The Labour Force in Docklands

	Manual/ unskilled	*Rank London*	*% Professional*	*Rank London (from lowest)*
Tower Hamlets	11.6	1	7.1	1
Southwark	10.9	2	10.9	5
Newham	8.7	3	7.8	2

SOURCE: *London Labour Plan.*

The hardest people to find jobs for are the long-term unemployed as skills change and employers tend to select younger candidates. But even school leavers have been very hard hit. The same boroughs again produce some of the worst figures in London (Table 6.2).

TABLE 6.2
Unemployment in Docklands

	Long-term unemployed		*18 year olds u/e over 6 months*	
	%	*Rank*	*%*	*Rank*
Tower Hamlets	47.4	1	46.4	1
Southwark	45.3	3	46.0	2
Newham	43.7	5	45.3	4

SOURCE: MSC Intelligence Unit, *Bulletin*, Summer 1986.

Manufacturing in the area had followed the national trend of decline but the setting up of the LDDC did not stem the tide, indeed the situation grew worse. The changing pattern of land use made the riverside sites desirable residential areas and therefore land values rose dramatically. When an acre could be sold for £1 million the temptation became too great and firms sold up. These were the firms which employed the locals. In fact 3000 jobs were lost from the area, a greater number than those newly created.

The LDDC has not helped the unemployment problem greatly. The rate of unemployment has fallen slightly in Docklands but more slowly than the rest of London.

Table 6.3 shows that most of the firms coming into the area were relocating from another site so many of their employees simply came with them. This, of course, generated few new jobs for local people who, anyway, did not have the appropriate skills.

As Skillnet was not established until 1986, opportunities to train the unemployed were slow in coming. As more people are encour-

TABLE 6.3
Job Creation in Docklands

Jobs transferred from outside LDDC	5059
Jobs newly created	2838
Total	7897

SOURCE: LDDC.

aged to take courses and more school leavers are involved in compacts, jobs will become more accessible to the residents of Docklands.

It will also take time for subsidiary service industries, such as shopping and catering, to develop and these will open more opportunities for the unskilled.

Housing

The LDDC originally made a commitment that housing would be available for council tenants to buy at 'affordable prices' which, in the early days, was £40 000. Approximately 2000 houses were sold on this basis despite the fact that a purchaser would need a salary of £12 000 a year to get a mortgage of £35 000.

The scheme has been a victim of Docklands' success. Because of its proximity to central London, the demand for houses has been so great that prices have risen rapidly. A house that was bought at £40 000 could quickly be sold for £150 000. Land prices have risen because of the growing demand for housing so it has become difficult to allocate some homes for sale at lower prices (Figure 6.1).

The latest technique to make housing available has been to sell land to developers on the condition that they build some houses for the public sector to rent. But there is still considerable unrest as new luxury homes are built while the local resident faces problems related to the quality of local councils' housing stock.

FIGURE 6.1
The Effect of Demand and Supply on House Prices

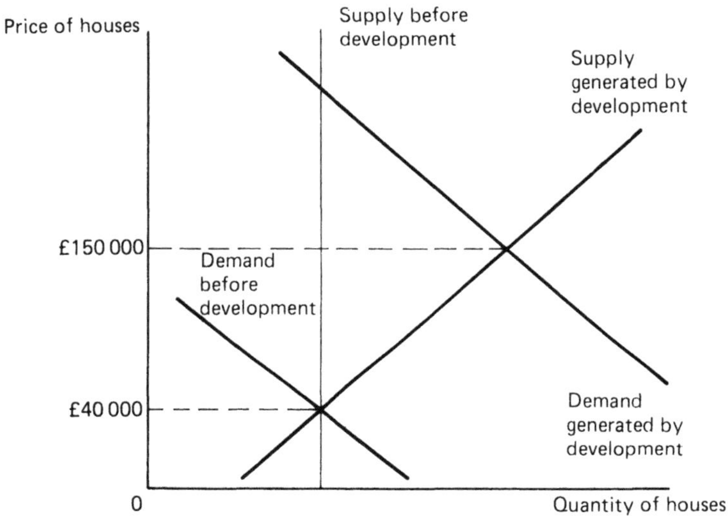

Local democracy

The local councils have always claimed that their role has been usurped. A great deal of resentment has been generated by the fact that outsiders came in with new powers and more money to cope with the problems of the area. The action groups which have been set up to coordinate local opposition have always claimed that if the same powers and resources had been given to the local councils, they would have done as well but taken more account of the needs of local people.

As time has passed the two factions have started working together more effectively, although it still seems that local people are suspicious of the workings of the LDDC. Skillnet is an example of the progress that has been made and it reflects the increasing recognition of the social role of the corporation.

The councils have also recognised the fact that they will be unable to stem the flow of development so they must make the most of it.

COUNCIL AGREES ROYAL DOCKS DEAL

Labour controlled Newham Council in East London has buried its differences with the LDDC and has reached an important agreement to cooperate with the commercial development of the borough's Royal Docks.

Council leaders hope the deal will yield up £100m of benefits from the corporation and developers. The wide-ranging agreement is a breakthrough in the LDDC's often strained relations with local authorities since the government set it up in 1981. It marks a shift in the political climate as urban development corporations are set up around the country.

In return for council approval for roads and infrastructure work, the corporation will attempt to ensure that 1500 homes are built which are cheap to rent or buy. It will put £10m over two years into community projects such as schools, meeting places and environmental schemes – a figure which could eventually grow to £60m, although not all from LDDC coffers.

The two sides have agreed to try to ensure that 25 per cent of the jobs created in the borough will go to local people. This will involve identifying and catering for the training needs of potential employers.

The council may also be able to put some of its land assets into proposed developments, which would enable it to receive a proportion of the profits made by companies moving into the docks.

Newham Council expects criticisms from community groups that the deal does not provide enough benefits for local people and that the development of the Royal Docks could detract from East Ham and Stratford as shopping centres to the west.

However, the chairman of the council's joint planning and policy committees has told protesters: 'We are getting the best deal we can. These are not the crumbs from the table that we have been used to.'

Adapted from the *Financial Times*, 28th September 1987.

Has it worked?

The development of Docklands has created a confused picture of costs and benefits. It is a picture which varies dramatically according to who is painting it. The same question posed to a representative of the LDDC and a local borough elicits a very different response. The reason for these differences may stem from the way the LDDC was set up and expected to work. The powers that it was given enabled decisions to be taken with less consultation than was required previously and this did not smooth its path.

Secondly, it was an exercise in demand led planning. The LDDC put in infrastructure to encourage firms to want to move in. This process inevitably caused negative externalities for local people, both in the short and long term. Living in the midst of a major building development is not a pleasant experience, especially when there seems to be nothing in it for you.

The third problem was caused by the differing attitudes to planning on the part of the LDDC and the boroughs. Because of the multitude of social problems in the area, planning had tended to be needs-oriented. The demand led projects laid primary stress on getting industry in at all costs.

A fourth point is that although a lot of new firms have moved in, much of the existing industry has moved elsewhere so many of the jobs that suited the local population have disappeared. The LDDC recognises all the new jobs that it has created but the Docklands residents are more aware of their disappearing employment.

To sum up, the LDDC has been very successful in creating economic benefit, but this has been at the expense of the social costs that have been incurred. As the ten-year life of the corporation draws to its close, it will be more possible to assess whether the initial concern with economic development has led to a long-term improvement in social conditions. The most fruitful way forward for the boroughs seems to be to ensure that they negotiate a good deal with the developers in order to reap the maximum benefit for the local residents.

Wigan Pier: A Small-scale Development

At the other extreme of development from Docklands, both in location and approach, is the northern town of Wigan.

Wigan is a typical product of the industrial revolution. It has long been the butt of music hall jokes and its image was not improved by George Orwell's graphic descriptions of living conditions in the poverty-stricken back-streets during the 1930s in his book *The Road to Wigan Pier*. Coal and cotton had been the source of the town's wealth and their decline left a trail of unemployment and dereliction.

Instead of trying to forget the past, the town decided to make the most of it. The town's heritage lay in ruins along the Leeds and Liverpool Canal. The 'pier' which George Orwell claimed not to be able to find, is a jetty which was used to load coal into barges for the journey to Liverpool.

A major project was established to return the pier and surrounding warehouses to their former glory. The scheme involved renovating the mill and the warehouses along the canal in order to provide a variety of resources for the town and a major tourist attraction. At the centre of the development is a living museum where actors portray the way of life in 1900. There is also a water bus, concert hall, exhibition space as well as catering and shopping facilities associated with tourism. One warehouse, a listed building dating from 1777, has been converted into prestige office space. Another building is used as an education centre which provides a base for both local and regional visits.

The Trencherfield Mill was on the point of closure when the scheme was initiated. The council bought it and the firm became its tenant and occupied the upper floor. This saved 130 jobs and since then 230 more people have been recruited. The building houses the concert and exhibition hall which also attracts trade promotions. Spare floor space is used by the fashion department of the local technical college which has made links with the textile firm above.

Benefits

- 330 new jobs on the site
- 140 new jobs created in local hotels and catering
- 130 jobs saved at Trencherfield plus 230 jobs created
- Adjacent land sold for commercial and industrial development
- Adjacent industries have cleaned up their properties
- New educational, entertainment and recreational facilities

The improvements can be summed up in the following statement from the planning department: 'The renewed confidence is certainly manifesting itself in the physical fabric and the economy of the area.'

Costs

The site on which the development took place was a derelict eyesore and an embarrassment to the town, so the costs in terms of land was minimal.

The plan was to take three years and cost £4 million. The initial investment came from the private sector but Wigan put up some of the money in order to attract grants from a range of national donors and the EEC. Regional development and tourism were the primary interests of these agencies which contributed approximately 75 per cent of the cost.

Wigan itself invested approximately £1 million in the project. By looking at how else this might have been spent we can build a picture of the opportunity cost of the development.

Without the pier scheme the council would have had an extra £1 million to spend on roads, housing, education, etc. which would have given direct benefits immediately to residents of the town. The council was taking a longer term view by deciding to develop the pier, as they believed that by spending their money in this way they would attract more from other sources. The end result would mean that much more money would come into the town as the scheme progressed. The list of benefits suggests that their thinking was correct. Their investment would not, by itself, have gone very far if it had been used in the traditional way. Has the multiplier effect therefore helped generate new jobs and income which have helped the town recover from the effects of structural change?

Wigan's flagship project has been an audacious plan which has paid off.

A Comparison?

The revival of inner city areas often depends on a change of image. The failure of industry to take advantage of low rents and available labour force reflects this. New firms do not want to be associated with dereliction.

In Wigan, the local authority took the initiative and raised substantial funds for a project which they viewed as growth point for the town. The scheme created new jobs and a certain amount of investment. In itself this would have been insufficient to make much difference. The externalities were more important. Many visitors came and discovered that Wigan didn't live up to the picture they had of it. The psychological effect on the town was substantial and this new image encouraged new firms and shops to move in.

In Docklands, private funding was the order of the day after a relatively small amount of public money was initially injected. Although the scale was smaller, Wigan probably had the more difficult problem on its hands. Stimulating growth in the North West was a challenge because the cities of Liverpool and Manchester were already trying to revive their economic standing. The area designated for development in London was a short distance from the financial centre of the City which has some of the highest rents in the world. The availability of purpose-built offices, equipped for the latest technology, would therefore be an almost guaranteed success.

The scale of the exercise and the state of demand are both key factors in determining the best solution to a problem of inner city decay. In both cases, initial funding from the public sector has been a stimulus to the private sector but Wigan had to invest proportionately more in order to stimulate demand. The Docklands scheme was on a much larger scale and public funds could not have paid the bill, but as demand was there a relatively small injection was sufficient to get things going. If inner city regeneration is going to be successful in the long run, schemes must be economically viable. Otherwise, they will have to be supported indefinitely by public money.

Regional Policy 7

NORTH–SOUTH DIVIDE GAPES TOWARDS THE YEAR 2000

Hopes that the next decade will witness the elimination of the deep economic gulf between North and South are likely to be sorely disappointed.

Even though labour shortages in London and the South East will force some decentralisation of economic activity to neighbouring regions, more distant areas, with the exception of Wales, are unlikely to benefit, concludes a study by Cambridge Econometrics and Northern Ireland Economic Research on regional economic prospects.

The report predicts: 'The future is expected to resemble the 1950s when the peripheral regions languished, more than the 1960s and 1970s when strong government regional policy measures brought a revival to the peripheral.'

The report also concludes that the line dividing the prosperous South from the slow growing North still begins at the Severn Estuary but has shifted in a more north-easterly direction so that the Midlands is now included in the South. Even so the division shows no sign of being eradicated in the 1990s.

One of the main assumptions of the report, which is one of the few to project economic trends to the end of the century, implies that regional policies could redistribute prosperity more evenly throughout the country. While the report's authors are careful to avoid such an explicit conclusion and there is scarce evidence that regional policy brought about any lasting transfer of wealth in the past, the suggestion remains. The study appears to demolish the government's assumption that economic growth will eventually radiate out to all the regions.

While there is little evidence for the government's case, the study does indicate that for some regions, like the East and West Midlands, East Anglia and some extent Wales, have benefited from expansion in the South and will continue to do so. Of all the regions the Midlands will grow most rapidly, expanding 49.4% between 1987 and 2000.

Moreover, the report projects that economic growth will average 2.4% a year during the 1990s, after slower growth up to 1992. But that is well below the current level of growth of productive capacity of around 3 to 3.5%. And if the current investment boom is sustained, the ability of the country to grow without inflaming inflation could increase.

Adapted from *The Independent*, 3 January 1989.

Unemployment, standard of living, house prices and the level of investment are some of the variables which help us to form an economic picture of a region. In order to decide whether the north–south divide really exists we need to compare such data for different parts of the country. The term 'north' will be used to cover areas that lie north of a line from the Severn to the Wash. When the country is broken down into regions North refers to northern England.

Unemployment

Unemployment rose throughout the country between 1975 and 1986, but it affected some regions more severely. Table 7.1 shows the disparity. London and the South East suffered less than half the unemployment rate of the North and Northern Ireland. We must look more closely to see if the position of the north, in general, has deteriorated further than the south. A comparison of the ratio of unemployment to the national average will tell us if the gulf is getting wider. These do not give us a simple answer because some regions of the north have fared worse than others but on average unemployment in the south has risen less.

Since 1986 unemployment has started to fall. Table 7.2 shows that although levels have fallen everywhere the change has been more significant in the south than the north.

Standard of Living

Standard of living can be compared by looking at a variety of data.

TABLE 7.1
Unemployment, 1983–8

Region	*1983*	*1984*	*1985*	*1986*	*1987*	*1988*
United Kingdom	10.5	10.7	10.9	11.1	10.0	8.0
Northern Ireland	15.5	15.9	16.1	17.6	17.6	16.4
Scotland	12.3	12.6	12.9	13.3	13.0	11.2
North	14.6	15.3	15.4	15.2	14.0	11.9
North West	13.4	13.6	13.8	13.9	12.7	10.7
Wales	12.9	13.2	13.8	13.9	12.5	10.5
Yorks & Humberside	11.4	11.7	12.0	12.4	11.3	9.5
West Midlands	12.9	12.7	12.7	12.6	11.1	8.5
East Midlands	9.5	9.8	9.9	9.9	9.0	7.2
South West	8.7	9.0	9.3	9.5	8.2	6.3
South East	7.5	7.8	8.0	8.2	7.1	5.2
East Anglia	8.0	7.9	8.0	8.1	6.8	4.8

SOURCE: Department of Employment, *Regional Trends* (HMSO, 1989).

The selection in Table 7.2 identifies the main differences across the country.

Data on income and expenditure must be interpreted with care. The proportion of a region's income which comes from social security reflects the level of unemployment and dependents. A high level suggests relatively low output and growth. High expenditure on housing, etc. may offset high earnings.

The amount a household earns may be high but if unavoidable expenditure, for example, on housing is also high they may benefit little from high earnings. A family living in the South East will be worse off than a family with the same earning in the North West because the same three-bedroomed semi costs at least twice as much.

The standard of living is also reflected in how people spend their

TABLE 7.2
Regional Differences in Standard of Living
(A) Income and Expenditure

Region	*Average weekly household income*	*Average weekly household expenditure*	*% of income from social security benefits*	*% of total expenditure on housing*
United Kingdom	245.2	183.2	12.5	16.5
North	197.2	150.2	16.9	15.1
Wales	207.2	163.6	18.1	14.1
Northern Ireland	207.8	178.5	19.3	12.5
Yorks & Humberside	209.5	157.3	15.3	15.6
Scotland	212.5	161.8	15.4	13.6
East Anglia	220.5	188.2	13.5	15.4
West Midlands	225.3	166.4	14.4	16.9
East Midlands	226.9	169.8	13.7	16.7
North West	231.9	172.0	14.4	16.3
South West	250.9	189.5	11.9	16.8
South East	302.1	219.2	8.6	18.0

(B) Durable Goods

Region	*% of households having:*		
	Telephone	*Deep freezer*	*Dishwasher*
United Kingdom	82	69	6
Northern Ireland	72	46	6
North	74	63	3

TABLE 7.2 *contd*
Regional Differences in Standard of Living
(B) Durable Goods contd

Region	*% of households having:* Telephone	*Deep freezer*	*Dishwasher*
Wales	75	67	4
West Midlands	76	64	5
Yorks & Humberside	79	63	4
Scotland	80	59	5
North West	81	68	5
East Midlands	82	71	6
South West	84	74	7
East Anglia	85	74	8
South East	88	74	9

SOURCE: Department of Employment, *Regional Trends* (HMSO, 1989).

(C) Regional Distribution of Adults Taking Holidays (percentage)

Region	*Adults taking no holiday*	*Holiday in Britain*	*Holiday abroad*
North	6	5	5
Yorks & Humberside	9	10	19
East Midlands	6	9	7
East Anglia	3	4	3
Greater London	13	10	15
Rest of South East	15	19	23
South West	8	8	8
West Midlands	10	10	8
North West	15	12	10
Wales	5	5	6
Scotland	11	8	7
Total	100	100	100

SOURCE: Department of Employment, *Regional Trends* (HMSO, 1988).

money. The data shows that more people in the south have freezers, telephones and dishwashers. They also take more holidays.

All this information confirms the divide. Even if people in the south have to pay much more for their housing they have plenty left over for consumer durables and making the most of their leisure time. The problems are not uniformly spread as there are pockets of wealth in the north and poverty in the south but they do not have a significant effect on the overall picture.

Migration

The evidence from Table 7.3 shows a north to south flow of population which confirms the hypothesis of a divide. People are leaving the poorer areas of the north to find jobs in the south. The data suggests that Greater London is the only area of the south

TABLE 7.3
Inter-regional Movements (Thousands)

Region	*Movements in*	*Movements out*	*Net migration*
Greater London	170	243	−73
North West	82	110	−28
Scotland	48	62	−14
North	47	54	−7
Northern Ireland	10	15	−5
West Midlands	93	95	−2
Yorks & Humberside	87	88	−1
Wales	64	50	+14
Rest of South East	300	282	+18
East Midlands	106	87	+19
East Anglia	83	51	+32
South West	151	105	+46

SOURCE: Department of Employment, *Regional Trends* (HMSO, 1989).

which is losing people as they move out to the south east. However, very recent data suggests that even this trend has been reversed as developments like Docklands attract people back into the city. Much of the movement in the south east and London comes from people relocating within the region. The figures are relatively stable because people from the north find it almost impossible to move to the south east. Additions to population are occurring in the next band. East Anglia, the East Midlands and the South West offer proximity to London, good communications and lower land prices. It is in these areas that new industries are setting up. The hi-tech or sunrise industries have focused on East Anglia and the Thames Valley. Table 7.4 shows that more new firms are being registered in the south than the north.

TABLE 7.4
Business Registrations and Deregistrations (Thousands)

Region	*Registrations*	*Deregistrations*	*Net gain*
United Kingdom	1416.4	1192.0	224.4
Northern Ireland	27.9	20.7	7.3
North	51.1	44.9	6.2
Wales	60.7	52.4	8.3
East Anglia	51.9	41.8	10.1
North West	139.3	128.8	10.5
Yorks & Humberside	104.2	92.3	11.9
Scotland	88.3	74.9	13.4
East Midlands	91.9	76.3	15.6
West Midlands	120.1	102.8	17.3
South West	124.2	101.6	22.6
South East	556.9	455.5	101.4

SOURCE: *Regional Trends* (HMSO, 1989).

Investment

As new firms set up in the south, the level of investment is relatively much greater. The declining industries of the north mean that there is little investment. The lack of growth creates little demand for new machinery and when existing stock wears out it does not need to be replaced.

Hi-tech industries abound in the south, although the offices and factories are more concerned with research and development and the production of software. Most of the large companies have their manufacturing plants in Scotland and Northern Ireland and other areas where they can benefit from regional assistance.

A North–South Divide?

In general, the data supports the hypothesis of the north–south divide. There are, however, suggestions that the boundary of the south is moving further north than the line from the Severn to the Wash. The East Midlands is among the regions that are demonstrating growth and falling unemployment but the standard of living still lags behind the richer areas. Figure 7.1, which shows the Gross Domestic Product per head for each region, confirms the divide and shows the East Midlands among the richer areas.

Why is There a North–South Divide?

The north has always been a stronghold of manufacturing. Its wealth grew from coal, iron and steel and other heavy industries. Deindustrialisation has changed the industrial structure of the country. The UK has moved through the stages of development from an agrarian to a manufacturing economy and is now more than two-thirds dependent on the tertiary sector.

There is a great deal of statistical evidence to confirm the decline of manufacturing. Table 7.5 shows a selection of this data. A key indicator is manufacturing's contribution to gross domestic product which has fallen steadily as the service sector's contribution has risen.

Part B of the table shows the amount of investment in the two sectors as a percentage of total investment. There has been a steady fall in the manufacturing industry's share, although the boom during the latter half of the 1980s led to a revival. The service sector

FIGURE 7.1
Gross Domestic Product Per Head as a Percentage of the UK Average[1]

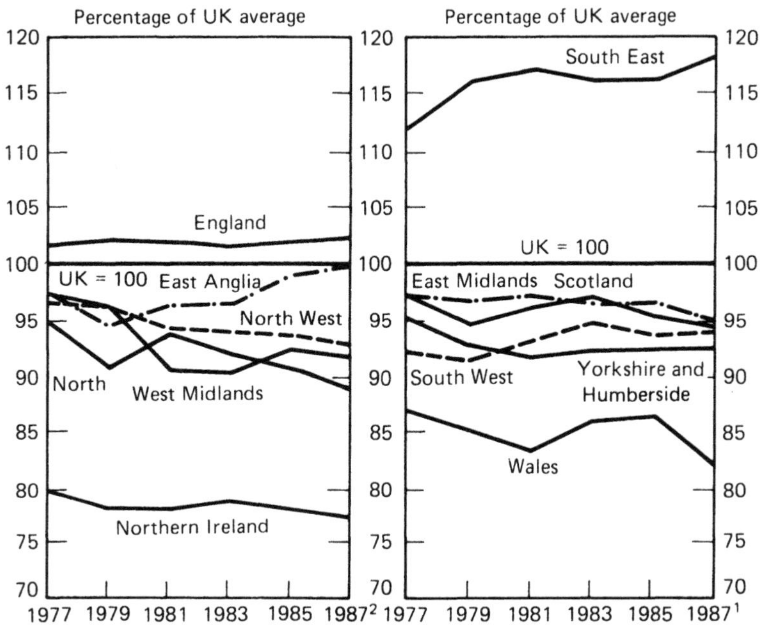

[1] Provisional
SOURCE *Regional Trends* (HMSO, 1989).

exhibits a consistent rise both in its share and in the total amount of investment, despite the recession of the early 1980s. The fall in employment in manufacturing compared with the rise in the service sector is an important consequence of the changing pattern. Because of the concentration of manufacturing industry in the north the decline has had more serious repercussions in both economic and human terms. The unemployment rate has been consistently higher and all types of resources have been under used.

TABLE 7.5

(A) Manufacturing and Service Industry: Share of Output (percentage of GDP at factor cost)

Year	Manufacturing	Service
1964	42.8	51.2
1969	41.4	54.1
1973	39.8	56.1
1979	34.8	58.4
1982	31.1	59.7
1987	28.7	62.3

(B) Manufacturing and Service Industries: Investment (percentage of gross domestic fixed capital formation)

Year	Manufacturing	Service
1977	17	20
1979	18	21
1981	13	25.5
1983	12	26.5
1985	14	30
1987	14	30

(C) Manufacturing and Service Industries: Employment (000s)

Year	Manufacturing	Service
1971	8065	11 627
1979	7253	13 580
1981	6222	13 468
1986	5236	14 486
1988	5097	15 212

SOURCE: Department of Employment, *Social Trends* (HMSO, 1989).

Industrial Location: Influences on the Existing Pattern

The pattern of British industry today still reflects its historical origins to some extent. The coalfields were the dominant factor and heavy industry is still located in these areas. Sources of raw materials and power had a strong pull for industry but today this has changed. Power is readily available throughout the country and transport is faster so industrialists can take other factors into account. They are aiming to reduce their private costs and look for sites which combine all their needs for the lowest cost.

Some industries still find the proximity of raw materials a draw. If the process uses large volumes of a raw material but leaves much of it as waste – in other words, it is bulk reducing – the firm is likely to locate close to the source. A firm which adds to the bulk of raw materials will, on the other hand, want to be close to its market. Making lemonade, which adds litres of water to a small volume of raw materials, is better off near the market because there is no point in carrying water around the country when it is available everywhere. In the end, the decision will depend on the costs of transport relative to other factors. If transport is cheap and quick, other factors, like the cost of land or the availability of labour, will be more important.

Some industries have to be located in isolated areas. The fear factor means that nuclear power stations were set up, in general, in the more remote parts of Britain. They also need a great deal of water so they tend to be by the sea. Industries which need good transport links are usually close to motorways. The planning battles over the M25 interchange sites reflect the importance of the market to many firms.

As trade unions make national pay agreements in Britain, wage differentials tend not to be a strong influence. A firm may, in fact, be prepared to pay above the national rate in areas of labour shortage in order to avoid moving. This is usually because they have a labour force trained for the job and other factors which dominate their choice of location. Firms which have been in one area for a long time will have built up links and contacts which are more important to them than the savings they might make in a new location. Many small firms are established in an area simply because the owner lives there. If they grow, the economics of their location may not be sound, unless their close links with the locality outweigh other factors.

Regional Policy

The UK has had a regional policy since 1934. The depression of the 1930s first showed that there was a need for aid in the areas which were worst hit. Ever since then the aim of the policy has been to attract industry to areas of high unemployment by providing grants and tax incentives, in other words, by taking work to the workers.

The motivation for the policy is both social and economic. The problems relating to areas of high unemployment are severe and involve all the social side-effects mentioned in other chapters. Health, education, the environment all suffer in areas with high unemployment. The spiral of decline repels potential investors and therefore makes development more unlikely.

The economic reasons stem from the waste of resources. If people, factories and other factors of production are lying idle, the economy cannot be producing on the boundary of its production possibility curve (Figure 7.2). It must therefore be failing to produce all the goods that it can.

Regional Policy: Past and Present

Policy in the past

Between the 1930s and the 1970s regional policy developed a carrot and stick approach to industry. The carrot was in the form of subsidies offered to companies to set up in development areas designated by the government. Trading estates were established and factories built to entice firms into these areas. Strict regulations which limited industrial development in the South East and the West Midlands were the stick.

These policies met with mixed success. Some areas undoubtedly benefited from the subsidies. Wales had a net gain of 444 new firms and Scotland won 228.

Not all firms, however, could be persuaded to move to the

FIGURE 7.2
Production Possibility Curve: Wasted Resources

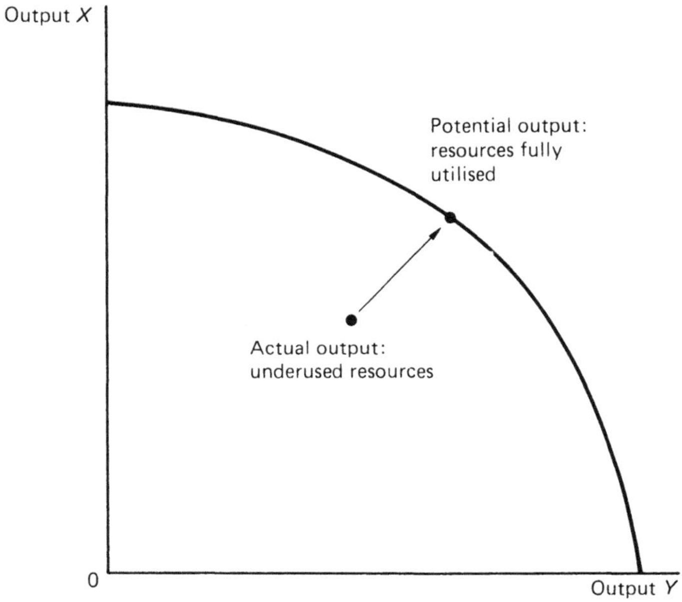

development areas, even with subsidies. The result was that the unexpected winners from this policy were East Anglia and the South West who respectively had a net gain of 325 and 269 new firms. These were probably firms which wanted to expand in the South East or the West Midlands but were refused permission. These two regions were therefore the nearest alternative.

The success of regional policy is not easy to judge because it is difficult to tell what would have happened without it. Structural change and government policy were working in opposite directions. The policy was unlikely to reverse the trend of change but helped to reduce its effect.

By the end of the 1970s research suggests that about 500 000 jobs had been created in the development areas. This figure includes an allowance for the regional multiplier, an adjustment which takes into account the knock on effect of creating new jobs. If every new factory which is set up buys goods in the area, more demand will be created which will lead to more new jobs. All the extra people who are employed will also have more to spend so they will raise demand as well. The regional multiplier tries to calculate the final value of an injection of new investment and new jobs into an area. Unfortunately, not all new firms have a strong multiplier effect. A new car plant, for example, may bring in skilled people who send money home to their families elsewhere. It will also import components and raw materials from their plants in other parts of the country and will export their profits out of the region when they sell the cars. In total, the addition to the local economy will be from the unskilled labour that they employ. Over time there may be improvements as they train more local people for skilled jobs but unless it is an industry which can use lots of local resources, the effects may not be great.

The policy has its limitations because firms may be enticed to locations with financial incentives but where costs are actually higher. As long as grants are available they can survive but when the subsidies cease their cost structure cannot cope with competition in the market. Equally, when the market takes a downturn the factories which a firm shuts first tend to be the peripheral ones in development areas. A depression therefore hits these regions hardest.

The negative aspects of such a policy may thwart economic growth. A firm which wants to expand in prohibited areas may have many reasons for not wanting to move. These may range from solid economics to lethargy but the result will be a loss of potential output.

Cost is also a problem. In the 1970s, £5000 million was spent on regional policy. It has been estimated that every job created directly by the policy cost £50 000.

Policy in the 1980s

In a search to use resources effectively the new government brought changes to regional policy. The aim had been to create jobs in the regions but giving grants for investment had encouraged capital intensive industries to develop in areas of high unemployment. What they really needed was labour intensive industry. As a result the grants became linked to job creation.

The grants also became discretionary because they were being given to firms which would have developed anyway instead of to those that needed encouragement. Giving grants to oil companies for exploiting the North Sea was not a good use of limited resources.

As service industries became the focus of growth in the economy they became eligible for grants. Small firms became the centre of attention, receiving both financial help and advice from various government agencies.

The government also felt that the money had been spread too thinly and so reduced the areas where assistance was available from a coverage of 35 to 15 per cent of the working population.

These changes are likely to make the policy more cost effective but they have been accompanied by a reduction in government spending from £700 million to £400 million between 1984 and 1988 and a steady decline is expected in future.

This policy change has taken place because the government has a free market approach to regional policy, and suggests that if the market is allowed to function freely it will remove the disparities between regions.

Firms should be permitted to move as they wish because if they see cheap land and labour they will take advantage of it. If they do not there must be economic disadvantages which outweigh the advantages so the government should not intervene. Intervention would lead to an inefficient allocation of resources as the firm would be located where costs are higher.

Labour should be treated in the same way. If people are dissatisfied with the jobs and standard of living locally, they will move elsewhere. This will reduce local unemployment so wages will rise and therefore the standard of living will improve. If workers move to areas with a shortage of labour, supply will increase and wages will fall until there is equilibrium. Eventually, there will be no regional disparities unless workers think that an area has advantages which outweigh the shortage of jobs, and again the government should not intervene as it would distort the market.

The problem with this theory is that it assumes that the market is perfect and adjustments will automatically take place. In fact the market is far from perfect and many factors will prevent this adjustment.

An Imperfect Economy

National wage bargaining has led to similar wage levels throughout the country, whatever the local rate of productivity or unemployment. Areas of high unemployment do not have a wage advantage to attract new industry. Firms are just as concerned by how much people produce as the amount it has to pay them.

The provision of unemployment benefit and social security means that the advantages of staying in the region with high unemployment are likely to outweigh all the costs of moving.

When a firm is looking for a new location, it will be concerned about its private costs. It will not be concerned about the welfare of the community as a whole. By moving to an area where there is already congestion social costs will rise. There will be more pressure on transport and labour costs may be pushed up as there is more competition for employees.

The theory assumes that firms investigate alternative new locations carefully. In fact research shows that they have a list of minimum requirements and take the first site which meets it. They do not look for the perfect solution.

If people move to find work, they will increase demand for housing, health care, education and all the other social facilities. The cost of provision will rise or the services will deteriorate. The areas that they leave will have underutilised resources and the cost per head of keeping them going will increase.

Moving to a new area incurs costs. Buying and selling a house can cost £10 000 and moving a firm will be a great deal more. Disrupting family life has its costs which are difficult to measure but may result in distress which does have economic consequences. Divided families, caused by the breadwinner leaving to work in another part of the country, can develop a range of social problems. The family may be unable to follow because they cannot afford to buy a house in the south or can't exchange their council house for one in the new location.

The free market approach implies that eventually the market will clear and there will be no regional inequalities. What is not clear is how long this will take.

The regional multiplier implies that rich areas will get richer and poor areas poorer if they are left to their own devices. As people move to the rich areas to get jobs, the total spending power increases through the multiplier to make the region richer still. As these people leave the poor areas spending power falls, the multiplier exaggerates the declining situation and the region becomes less and less attractive to new industry.

There are deep-rooted reasons for regional inequalities. Structural change from the sunset to the sunrise industries means that requirements are different. The old industries were coalfield based and therefore tied to their location, the new hi-tech industries are much more footloose but tend to want to be nearer to their customers. These trends cannot be overcome simply by relying on the market. Adjustment is a slow process and may well never be achieved.

Do We Need Regional Policy?

There are drawbacks associated with both regional policy and the free market approach. The article at the beginning of the chapter poses both sides of the argument. There are economists claiming that a much stronger regional policy is the only possible solution, while others suggest that the policies of the 1970s had little effect.

Clearly, the policies of the past may not have led to the best allocation of resources as firms have been encouraged to move to areas which are not the most cost effective. It may, however, have minimised waste because more of the resources of the declining regions have been used by the firms which have been attracted into these areas.

The failure of market forces prevents structural change from solving unemployment. At best, the period of adjustment can be very lengthy.

The government must have policies to cushion the effect of the change. Currently, 0.2 per cent of GDP is being spent on regional policy which is insufficient to make much difference. The policy is concentrating on small areas and relying on the trickle-down effect. If the inner city areas and the enterprise zones are developed it should spark further investment in the region as a whole. As long as the economy is buoyant and there is a desire to invest this may work. If there is a downturn interest will be lost.

The effectiveness of regional policy is much influenced by the state of the rest of the economy. Increasing wealth and rising employment mean that demand is rising. Investment will then increase because industry wants to make the goods which people want to buy. When investment is rising in the country generally, firms will be attracted by the incentives offered in the regions. If the reverse is happening and there is little investment these incentives will have little effect.

Continued economic growth is essential if the north–south divide is to be narrowed.

Whatever the costs and benefits of the two sides of the argument, the decision in the end will be a value judgement.

Some may believe that the market will work and the divide will gradually be overcome because of price differentials and perhaps a small amount of government assistance. In this case, the costs incurred will be the hardship and waste of resources in the regions while the adjustments are made. The benefits will come from firms being located in the lowest cost location and therefore producing goods more cheaply. The economy will also be affected because the government will have to spend less.

Others may believe that the government should intervene and spend more to overcome the divide between the north and south. It is an issue of the relative benefits of government spending and the free market.

8

Income Distribution

THE ANGER OF EDDIE

Eddie Tyrell grew up in a street of twelve households in Liverpool's dockside – five of which had families out of work. His parents were not among the lucky ones. Now 21 and unemployed since he left school, Eddie is bitterly aware of how he was deprived when he was growing up: the lack of money, lack of clothes and, what really sticks in his mind, the lack of food.

'I laughed when I saw Ben Elton on the box joking about putting hot water on his cornflakes, because I used to do that,' Eddie said. 'I used to say to my sister: "I hate this house, there's never anything to eat." I used to cry.'

There are nearly a million young people under 19 who, like Eddie, are growing up in families where the head of the household is long-term unemployed. Most of them are trapped in pockets of poverty around the country, places which have missed out on the boom economy.

The Guardian, 4 May 1988.

The Other Side of the Picture

London W1

Stunning top floor
flat in prestigious
residential block
with lift and porterage.
Offering generous
accommodation
2 bedrooms with
ensuite bath and
shower rooms,
double reception,
dining room and
large kitchen-diner.

£959 000

PERSONALISED PLATES

KT 1 £25 000
11 RB £20 000
LOU 15 £24 500
BC 7 £20 500

Ideal gift for the
friend with everything

Paint-A-Pet

Professional artist will
paint your pet
A portrait for posterity
From £100
for 10" by 8" painting

Supa-Fast Car Sales

1978 FERRARI 512BB
White with red inserts
and red carpets
27 000 miles

£225 000

The article and adverts which introduce this chapter reflect the disparity of income and wealth in Britain. There is evidence to show that the poor are getting poorer and the rich richer. The growing differential is confirmed by data from the Family Expenditure Survey. Table 8.1 shows the population divided up into fifths or quintiles and tells us the proportion of total income each group

TABLE 8.1
Distribution of Original, Disposable and Final Household Income

	Quintile groups of households					
	Bottom fifth	*Next fifth*	*Middle fifth*	*Next fifth*	*Top fifth*	*Total*
Original income						
1976	0.8	9.4	18.8	26.6	44.4	100
1981	0.6	8.1	18.0	26.9	46.4	100
1985	0.3	6.0	17.2	27.3	49.2	100
1986	0.3	5.7	16.4	26.9	50.7	100
Disposable income						
1976	7.0	12.6	18.2	24.1	38.1	100
1981	6.7	12.1	17.7	24.1	39.4	100
1985	6.5	11.3	17.3	24.3	40.6	100
1986	5.9	11.0	16.9	24.1	42.2	100
Final income						
1976	7.4	12.7	18.0	24.0	37.9	100
1981	7.1	12.4	17.9	24.0	37.9	100
1985	6.7	11.8	17.4	24.0	40.2	100
1986	5.9	11.4	17.0	23.9	41.7	100

NOTE: *Original income* comes from earnings, pensions and investments.

Disposable income includes state benefits and excludes taxation.

Final income includes an amount which is statistically calculated to cover the benefit households gain from health, education and other government services. The cost of indirect taxes such as VAT and local taxation is deducted.

SOURCE Family Expenditure Survey (HMSO, 1987).

earns. The top fifth of the population gained progressively throughout the 1980s but the bottom three-fifths received a smaller proportion of total income. In the late 1980s the top category received over 40 per cent of total income while the bottom group had less than 6 per cent.

Table 8.2 tells us what has happened to the income of people in work. The five groups shown are selected as a representative cross-section of employment. All categories have gained in real terms since 1976 but the gain has varied in proportion. The differential has increased as the earnings of the top groups have risen more than those of the bottom groups. Clerical workers have also made significant gains as they have nearly caught up with mining and construction, the category ahead of them.

Those who are not working – single parents, the sick and disabled, pensioners and the unemployed – find themselves in the bottom quintiles of Table 8.1. The bottom two quintiles rely most heavily on state benefits. This can be seen in the difference between their original earnings and disposable income. Throughout the 1980s their disposable income fell. The unemployed were worst affected as supply-side policies encouraged people to take low-paid jobs.

TABLE 8.2
Average Gross Weekly Earnings for Adult Males

	Real earnings at 1986 prices			
Occupation groups	1976	1981	1985	1986
Professional, management and administration	235.0	249.2	278.5	298.2
Managerial (not general)	200.8	213.7	236.1	246.8
Construction and mining	164.7	164.7	165.4	172.6
Clerical	152.4	153.2	164.3	171.0
Farming and fishing	124.9	122.6	126.2	129.5

SOURCE: *New Earnings Survey*, 1987.

Why Do Such Disparities Exist?

Labour market demand

A business that wants to be as profitable as possible will have three things in mind when it decides how many people to employ. Their first interest will be in productivity, or how much each individual can produce with the machinery and equipment available. The amount that one person adds to total output is called the Marginal Physical Product (MPP). Beyond a certain point, each extra employee will add a little bit less to total output, if there is a fixed amount of capital.

FIGURE 8.1
How Many People Should the Firm Employ?

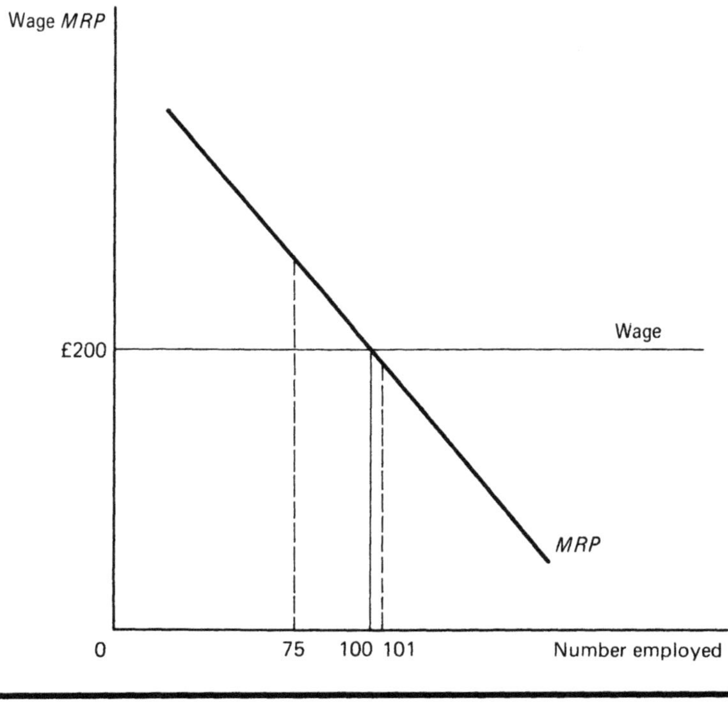

Secondly, they will look at the price at which they can sell their goods. The employer wishes to know the value of each worker's output. This is known as the Marginal Revenue Product (MRP) and can be calculated by multiplying the marginal physical product by the market price. If each worker is producing a little bit less the MRP will therefore fall.

In order to decide how many people to employ, the wage level must be taken into account. The perfect solution would be to employ more labour until the MRP is equal to the wage rate. This is demonstrated in Figure 8.1.

If the prevailing wage rate is £200 and the firm has no influence over it, the firm will continue to employ people until the MRP of the last employee is £200. If it chose to take on seventy-five people, it would be giving up the extra profit that could be made by the next twenty-five whose MRP was above the wage rate. If it employed 101, the last person would reduce his or her profit because of adding less to output than the £200 he or she cost in wages. The MRP curve, therefore, represents the demand curve for labour. This implies that if wages fall, more people will be employed and vice versa.

Should the price of the final product rise, the MRP for each employee will rise and the demand curve will shift to the right. Equally, the reverse will be true if the price fell. Figure 8.2 shows this effect. The implication of this is that the demand for labour is derived. Labour does not provide satisfaction like ordinary consumer goods, it is wanted for its ability to produce goods that can be sold at a profit. This suggests that wages should be higher in growth industries, where the products are in demand, than in the declining industries.

The theory assumes that markets are perfect and therefore the wage rate will settle at the equilibrium. As markets are full of imperfections and there have been significant changes in both supply and demand, the theory needs qualification.

Changing demand for the end product has had a serious effect on the demand for labour in some parts of the country. In steel, ship building and coal, the late 1970s and 1980s were a period when demand fell world-wide. The problem was compounded by industrialising countries which offered lower prices than Britain. The rate of unemployment therefore rose and incomes fell.

Technological change may mean that it is cheaper to use machinery than people. Declining demand combined with automa-

FIGURE 8.2
A Shift in the Demand Curve for Labour

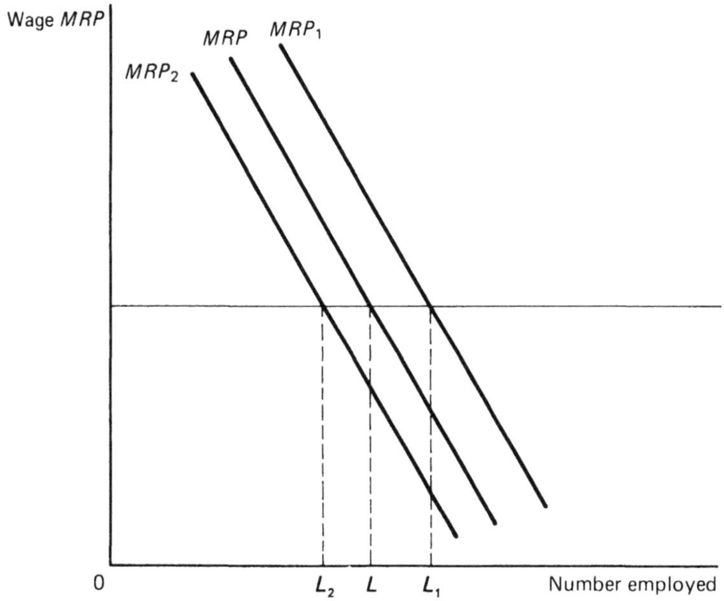

tion has led to a dramatic fall in employment in the coal industry. Production is now concentrated on a few, highly mechanised, efficient pits. Mines which could not use the new equipment because of narrow or faulted seams have been closed down with the resulting loss of jobs.

In the richer South East the trend has been reversed. The sunrise industries want to be close to their markets and have settled in and around London, creating a new demand for labour. As the region has become more affluent the demand for services has grown. Shops, offices and the leisure industry find it increasingly difficult to fill vacancies so they have to offer higher wages.

Changes in supply

The supply of labour is ultimately decided by the size of the working population. In the 1990s, the number of school leavers will fall substantially and as a result labour-intensive industries are getting worried about their future workforce. Not only are they starting schemes to attract new employees but they are attempting to bring women and the retired back to work.

Social trends also have a role to play. In the last thirty years the proportion of women who work has increased as attitudes have changed. The service sector is now trying to raise the figure further.

The government's supply-side policies aim to increase aggregate supply by increasing productivity and industrial growth. In order to encourage people to seek work, even at low rates of pay, benefits have become less generous and harder to get. This policy works provided that the jobs that become available match both the number and the skills of the unemployed. It is also dependent on the elasticity of demand for labour because lower wages should lead to more jobs being created. But if employers have a gloomy view of the future, nothing may persuade them to employ more people. If there is a skills mismatch and an inelastic demand for labour, these policies will result in more people falling into the poorest categories. Table 8.3 demonstrates the effect on the unemployed and other low-

TABLE 8.3
Proportions of Individuals in Households with Below-Average Income

	% with income below half the average			*% with income below 80% of the average*		
	1981	*1983*	*1985*	*1981*	*1983*	*1985*
Pensioner	6	5	7	66	60	66
Sick or disabled	21	16	19	74	61	70
Single parents	27	16	19	86	86	90
Unemployed	42	38	47	52	54	57
Other	13	18	14	52	54	57
Full-time worker	3	3	3	28	28	26

SOURCE: *Social Trends*, 1989.

paid groups. In 1983, 38 per cent of the unemployed earned less than half the average wage. By 1985, this figure had risen to 47 per cent.

The elasticity of supply is also crucial.

Supply cannot be changed rapidly in jobs which need a long training, so the more highly skilled the job, the more inelastic supply will be. The average job today needs more training so the appropriate labour force may take longer to recruit.

Difficulties in moving between areas or between jobs makes supply more inelastic. The higher cost of housing in the South East results in labour being less willing to move, thus the supply of labour becomes more inelastic and competing firms have to pay higher wages.

In a free market the combination of demand and supply should lead to the equilibrium price, in other words, the wage level. Markets are never perfect and therefore this rarely happens.

The labour market does not adjust instantly. When there is excess demand, employers rarely put wages up sufficiently to ensure that equilibrium is reached as they hope that rising costs can be limited. Shortages of labour may therefore persist for a long time.

The labour market suffers many other imperfections and during the 1980s it did not clear. Unemployment resulted. Government policy aimed to make it more perfect in order to allow wages to find a level at which supply will equal demand. Unemployment at this point is known as *voluntary unemployment* by supply-side economists because it is composed of people who are unwilling to take a job at this wage rate.

Let us first look at some of these imperfections and then at how the government has dealt with them.

Trade Unions

The role of trade unions is to improve conditions for their members. They hold pay negotiations with employers which result in the setting of minimum wages for the industry so both members and non-members benefit from their achievements.

If these minimum wages are above the equilibrium, the amount of labour employed may be reduced. Figure 8.3 shows how excess supply will be created. Wages start at the equilibrium level of £200 where 10 000 people are employed, after negotiations they rise to

FIGURE 8.3
Creating Excess Demand

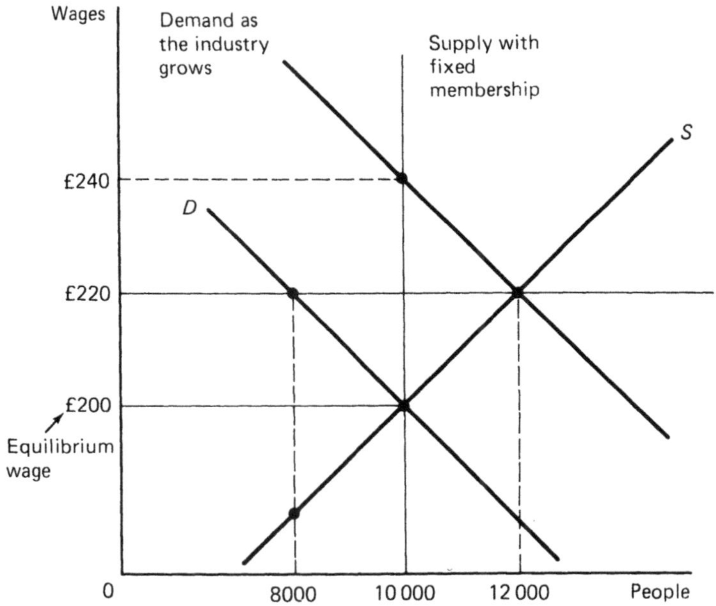

£220 but demand drops to 8000. This may lead to attempts to reduce the number eligible for membership by introducing restrictions.

As time passes the demand for this type of labour may rise. If the union has a fixed membership, there will now be excess demand and the wage level will rise to £240 to prevent a shortage in supply.

The ability to make the market imperfect has enabled unions to raise wage rates above the equilibrium. The degree to which this has been possible is difficult to calculate but estimates have been made. In general, it seems that a gain of between 10 and 20 per cent is common but in some occupations it can be as much as 50 per cent. As a result the distribution of income has moved in favour of trade union members.

During the 1980s the government passed a series of laws which were designed to reduce the power of the unions. The aim was to make the market work more freely and allow wages to find their equilibrium. Thus union members would no longer benefit from their ability to push wages up by limiting the supply of labour. The motives for these changes in the law have been both economic and political.

The abolition of the Dock Labour Scheme, for example, has been an associated attempt at making the labour market work more freely. The government's aim has been to remove restrictive practices which limit employment in the docks. The scheme was originally set up to give dockers permanent employment instead of being treated as casual labour. Membership of the scheme gave protection of employment and limited the dock labour force. The government argued that this restricted developments and a free market would therefore benefit future growth.

The professions also try to ensure that there is not a surplus. They restrict entry by long training periods and many exams. Barristers fought a ferocious battle when their monopoly of the courts was threatened.

Minimum Wage Legislation

It has always been difficult to run effective unions in industries like catering, retailing and the rag trade. Depressed wage levels have resulted because the workforce has not had the unifying force of the trade unions to improve conditions – allowing some employers to exploit their workers because they had monopsony power. This means that there is only one employer or for some reason employees are unable to move. As a result wages may be lower than in the free market. To prevent exploitation Wages Councils were established in order to set minimum wages. The argument for Wages Councils is both social and economic. Monopsonists are exploiting their power by paying a factor of production, usually labour, less than its value. The people who work in these industries have very little power or influence so employers can pay low wages and fail to provide the benefits they are entitled to. Setting a minimum wage ensures a degree of protection.

The strictly economic argument says that by imposing a minimum wage the number of people employed will fall as employers will have to pay above the equilibrium level. Figure 8.4 shows how excess supply develops when a wage above the equilibrium is imposed. At a wage of £100 there are 1000 jobs and the same number of people want to work. If legislation decrees that wages shall rise to £120, there will be 1200 looking for jobs, but only 800 available. So 800 will be better off but 200 people who were working before no longer have jobs. The actual change in employment will depend on whether the firm can pass the increased costs on to the consumer. In other words, if demand is inelastic, employment will stay much the same but if it is elastic, the number employed will fall.

The evidence is rather mixed. It appears that some groups do gain but others lose out. The ones that lose seem to be those who are already at the bottom of the heap, with neither skill nor experience on their side. This will lead to a redistribution of income in favour of the majority but will cause increased hardship for the minority.

FIGURE 8.4
The Effect of a Minimum Wage

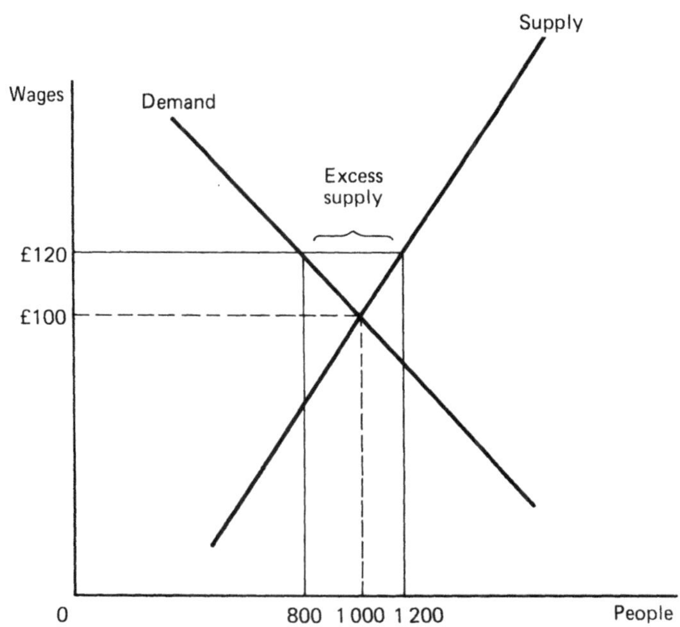

The government has abolished Wages Councils in order to make the market work more efficiently. This has caused considerable criticism because it has removed protection from the low paid, but the government believes that it will result in more people being employed.

Taxation

High levels of income tax will distort the labour market, according to the Laffer curve. People will be unwilling to work extra hours if they know that a high proportion of their extra earnings will be taken by the government.

FIGURE 8.5
The Laffer Curve

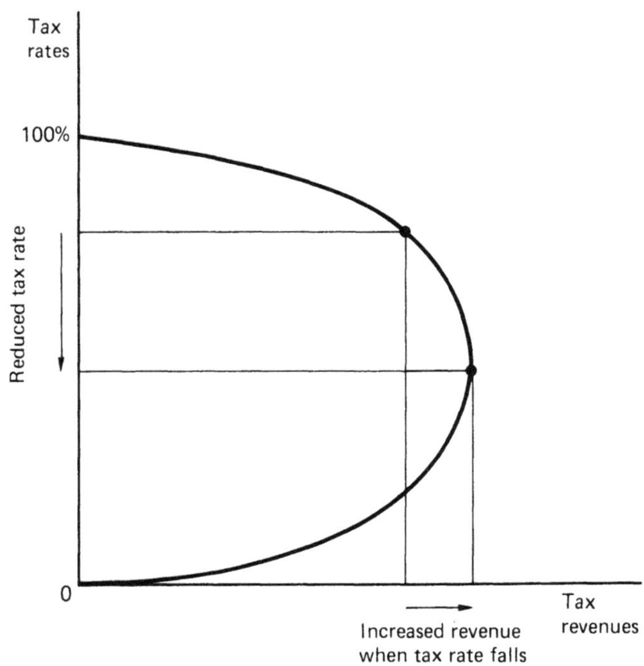

The curve shows that high tax rates reduce the government's revenue partly due to the disincentive effect but also because taxpayers will go to great lengths to disguise their earnings.

The government has followed the logic behind the Laffer curve and reduced income tax, especially the very high rates. Revenues have risen since the changes but this may be more to do with general economic growth than simply encouraging people to work more. If earnings rise, people pay more tax anyway.

If taxes are reduced, disposable income rises. This may have a disincentive effect because you have to work less to make the same amount. Equally, it makes leisure more expensive so more work may be done. The success of the policy will depend on whether the second example, the substitution effect, between work and leisure, outweighs the first example, the income effect to combine income with leisure.

Most of the working population is not in a position to vary the hours worked. Office jobs tend to be 9 to 5. Shops and factories may offer overtime but this is not a decision for the employee. The level of taxation may have some effect on top earners because they may have more flexibility and the changes have made a lot of difference to their take home pay.

This has, of course, led to changes in the distribution of income. Everyone who pays tax is keeping more of their income than they used to but the higher paid have gained more significantly, thus making the rich relatively richer.

The role of taxation seems to have changed from redistributing income to a supply-side policy tool.

Benefits

Britain has a system of benefits which is intended to protect people from the worst excesses of the market. Unemployment, sickness, family breakdown and other situations which cause individuals to forfeit their incomes from work cannot be dealt with simply by relying on the market. We have seen that most poverty is associated with non-work and society generally accepts that these people need help from the state. The level of assistance is more debatable. If benefits are low, income distribution will be more unequal.

The supply-siders would argue that there is little incentive for people to take low-paid jobs or the first job offered to them when they are unemployed if benefits provided by the state are too generous and continue for long periods. In order to overcome this, government policy has led to a tightening up of the rules on eligibility and the introduction of new systems of allocation.

A major problem, for a small minority of people, arose as a result of the 'poverty trap'. When an unemployed person takes a job, he or she is immediately subject to income tax and National Insurance payments. These can reduce earnings to such an extent that they are worse off than when they were unemployed. The effect was made less acute in the 1989 Budget by a change in the structure of National Insurance payments. The poverty trap still exists because if people lose benefits when they take a job, their total earnings may be reduced.

Imperfections and the Individual

Discrimination on the basis of age, sex, race and location can all make the market less than perfect for the individual. As an example, women have consistently earned less than men as Table 8.4 shows.

TABLE 8.4
Women's Earnings Relative to Men's

1970	63.1	1979	73.0	1984	73.5
1975	72.1	1980	73.5	1985	74.1
1976	75.1	1981	74.8	1986	74.3
1977	75.5	1982	73.9	1987	73.6
1978	73.9	1983	74.2	1988	75.1

SOURCE: *Employment Gazette*, November 1988.

In the early 1970s the relationship changed significantly but since then the situation has remained much the same. A variety of factors such as career breaks, part-time working and ties to one geographical location affect women's earning power. They are often not competing on equal grounds. Legislation outlaws discrimination on grounds of sex or race but it is very hard to police.

The factors mentioned so far detract from the individual's earning ability. There are others, however, which improve the prospects of higher pay.

Education and training were discussed in Chapter 3. Students accept a short-run reduction in earning power in order to earn more pay in the long run. Figure 8.6 shows how people with no qualifications are much more likely to be unemployed. This is particularly true of the young as they have no work experience to prove their ability.

Many people regard experience as more important than formal

FIGURE 8.6
Unemployment Rates Related to Qualifications

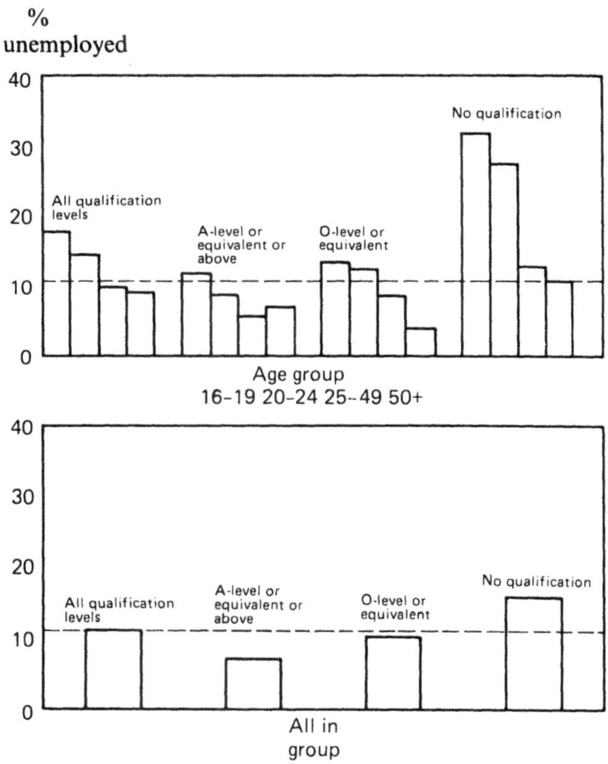

SOURCE: LFS estimates, *Employment Gazette*, October 1988.

qualifications because it shows what has already been achieved in work practice. Often, people with high earnings claim little success in education but they tend to have some particular aptitude which is in demand. Scoring goals in football, making a record that gets to Number One or an Oscar-winning performance in a film – none of these requires any paper qualifications but meets a demand. Since there is a shortage of such skills, in other words, because supply is inelastic, these people can earn an economic rent. Their income can be broken down into two parts. Transfer earnings are the wages that they would receive in their next best job and economic rent is the extra they earn because supply in their current job is limited. This relationship is shown in Figures 8.7 and 8.8.

FIGURE 8.7
If the Supply of Labour is Completely Inelastic Wages Equal Economic Rent

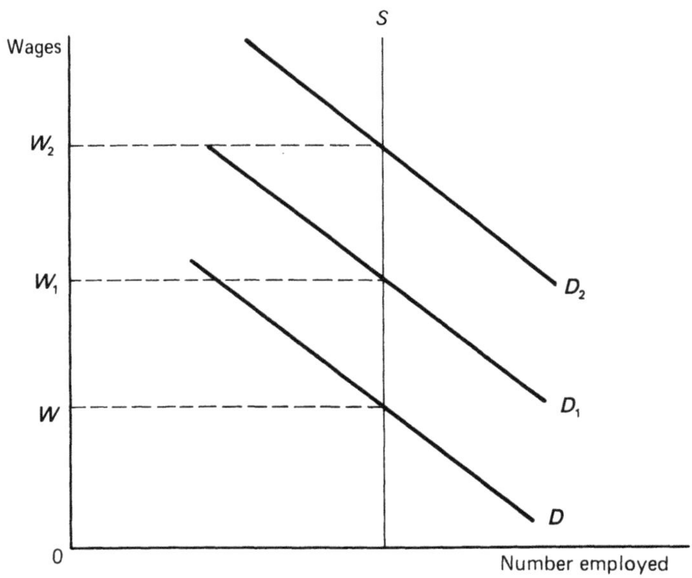

FIGURE 8.8
If the Supply of Labour is Inelastic Wages Equal Economic Rent Plus Transfer Earnings

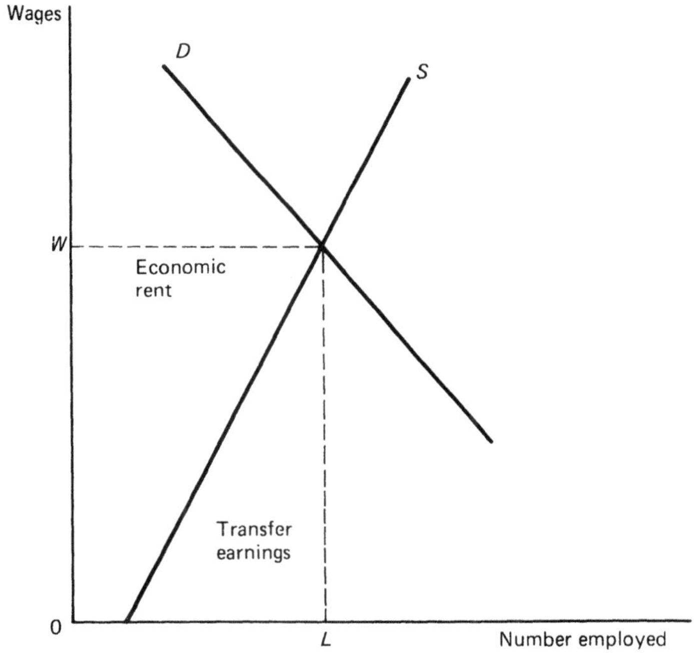

Wealth – a Source of Inequality?

The amount of wealth, or accumulated past income, that an individual holds both reflects and influences his or her income. But wealth can take different forms. The family who has bought a council house now has considerable 'wealth', but it may not help to increase their income and as interest rates rise it may become a positive liability. Owners of shares, land and other assets which we normally think of as 'wealth' gain because rent and interest add to their income. Rich people achieve their wealth through capital rather than labour earnings and many of them inherit it.

The data in Table 8.5 show how wealth is distributed among the top 50 per cent of the population. The growth of private and state pension rights has led to a more even spread but in 1985 the top 50 per cent still held between 81 and 85 per cent of wealth. Two figures are quoted because of the problem of allocating pension rights. The first figure shares them equally and the second assumes that if people own much marketable wealth, they will have higher pension rights.

The government regards direct taxation as a disincentive to work. Inheritance tax prevents families from passing all their wealth from one generation to the next and it therefore discourages people from earning and saving during their lifetimes. The levels of taxation on inheritance have been steadily relaxed, so with careful planning the burden of taxation can be significantly reduced by giving money and possessions away before death. Lord Montagu of Beaulieu, for example, has already passed a large proportion of his estate to his son. The upturn in the statistics for 1986 may reflect this change of pattern.

The Problem: Poverty

As the distribution of income becomes increasingly unequal the bottom fifth are becoming relatively poorer. The word poverty needs to be developed because the poorest person in the developed world is relatively well off compared with the poorest in the rest of the world. This reflects the difference between absolute and relative poverty.

In the introductory article Eddie loathed the poverty in which he lived but this was relative poverty. He is poor compared with the average for the rest of the country. He has cornflakes for breakfast but no milk to pour over them. If his poverty were absolute, he would have no cornflakes as they would be regarded as a luxury – in fact he would be lucky to have bread for breakfast.

Absolute poverty is usually regarded as the level of income necessary for bare subsistence so it will vary throughout the world according to climate, eating habits and the general cost of living.

Being poor leads to both social and economic disadvantage. All the other chapters have shown the problems associated with deprivation. A poor family is likely to suffer from all these problems and have little chance of escape. Inadequate housing and food leads to ill health, missed education and unequal chances in the jobs market.

The data in Table 8.6 which is taken from the Household Food,

TABLE 8.5
Distribution of Wealth (% and £ billion)

(i) Marketable Wealth

% of wealth	*1971*	*1976*	*1981*	*1985**	*1986**
owned by					
Most wealthy 1%	31	24	21	16	18
Most wealthy 2%	39	32	27	23	25
Most wealthy 5%	52	45	40	35	37
Most wealthy 10%	65	60	54	50	51
Most wealthy 25%	86	84	77	75	76
Most wealthy 50%	97	95	94	93	93
Total marketable wealth £ billion	140	263	546	906	1015

(ii) Marketable Wealth Plus Occupational and State Pension Rights

% of wealth	*1971*	*1976*	*1981*	*1985**	*1986**
owned by					
Most wealthy 1%	21	14	12	10	11
Most wealthy 2%	27	18	16	14	15
Most wealthy 5%	37	27	24	23	24
Most wealthy 10%	49	37	34	34	35
Most wealthy 25%	69–72	58–61	55–58	56–59	57–60
Most wealthy 50%	85–89	80–85	78–82	81–85	81–85

*Provisional
SOURCE: *Inland Revenue Statistics*, 1988.

Consumption and Expenditure Survey shows how spending on food varies according to income. The poorest group buys less of everything except eggs, a cheap source of protein. Fruit and vegetables, meat and fish all show how diet varies according to income.

TABLE 8.6
Consumption and Expenditure on Selected Food Items (pence per week)

		Income Group		
Expenditure	*A*	*B*	*C*	*D*
Milk and cream	118.48	107.82	104.34	93.95
Cheese	46.79	36.72	30.09	28.81
Meat and meat products	325.79	288.22	289.66	250.93
Fish	68.61	50.14	46.35	38.28
Eggs	18.15	18.50	19.68	20.83
Fats and oils	33.35	31.93	32.30	28.62
Sugar and preserves	18.62	14.60	15.85	15.62
Fruit and vegetables	272.42	219.65	196.88	164.45
Cereals (incl. bread)	188.33	167.30	164.65	147.85
Beverages	46.38	39.79	37.72	34.62
Other food	49.47	41.47	38.65	34.09
Total	£11.86	£10.16	£9.76	£8.85

SOURCE: *Household Food Consumption and Expenditure Survey*, 1987.

Can We Achieve Equity?

It is difficult to find a definition of equity that everyone would agree on. These are some of the alternatives:

- Income is distributed equally.
- No one has less than a minimum standard.
- Everyone gets what they need.
- Everyone gets what they deserve.
- If everyone has equal opportunity equity will result.
- If everyone agrees the system of allocation equity will result.

These differing views stem from differing value judgements. The extreme views are generally incompatible with achieving other goals like economic growth, efficiency, equity and liberty.

Equity of income distribution, as most people understand it, can never be achieved by the market alone. There will always be some people who have no means of earning a living. It is argued that the market will, in the long run, make everyone better off because it leads to economic growth. However large the National Income grows, the poor will only benefit if there are ways of redistributing this wealth to them.

BRITAIN LAGS BEHIND EC ON LOW-PAY THRESHOLD

Nearly half of Britain's adult employees are earning wages below the European 'decency threshold', according to the Low Pay Unit.

A report from the unit says that low-paid workers in Britain have completely missed out on the economic regeneration of the Thatcher decade.

The report, 'Ten Years On: The Poor Decade', shows the number of workers earning below the Council of Europe's threshold of £3.80 an hour has risen from 38 per cent of the workforce in 1979 to 47 per cent in 1989.

The unit says, 'The 1980s have been a decade of despair for the low paid and their families. The poorest fifth of male workers have increased their wages by 105 per cent, but the highest paid have had a 175 per cent rise.'

'This gap between the lowest and the average wage is bigger than it was a century ago.'

It also claims that progress towards equal pay came to a virtual standstill in the 1980s. In 1981 women earned 66.7 per cent of the average male wage, but by 1988 the figure had only increased to 67 per cent. Women in part-time jobs had particularly low hourly earnings.

The gap between young people's wages and those of adults also widened during the 1980s. Excluding those on government training schemes, one in ten 16 to 17 year olds earn less than £55 a week, and one in ten 18 to 20 year olds earn less than £77, says the unit. Older workers are not exempt from poverty wages. Sandro Nervo, a waiter in his forties, was earning £60 for a 62 hour week until he left his job more than a year ago. He is now suing the Paradiso E Inferno restaurant in London under the Wages Councils' regulations, which set minimum pay rates for the 2.5m workers in low-paid industries like catering and retail trade.

Mr Nerva should have been paid a minimum wage, which went up to £2 an hour just before he left. Instead, he says, he continued to be paid only 97p and is owed £16,201 by the restaurant. Three other waiters are also suing the company.

The government does not endorse the low-pay threshold. A spokeswoman for the Department of Employment said: 'Jobs are the best cure for poverty, and now there are more people in work than there were in 1979. To the best of our knowledge the decency threshold is not endorsed by any European country.'

Nine out of 12 European Community countries have statutory minimum wage provisions. By next year, Britain will be the only European country without a minimum wage.

The government is also opposed to calls by the EC for the introduction of a statutory minimum wage to aid market integration by 1992.

Adapted from *The Independent*, 2 May 1989.

How Can Income Be Redistributed?

A member of the government, when asked about poverty, said that jobs were the best cure. This is obviously true. The government's approach has been to make the market work more efficiently so the economy will grow. Unfortunately, this is a long process and a lot of people suffer while it happens. Earlier in the chapter we learnt that the poor tend to be those who cannot work and government policies to create jobs will therefore do little to help them. The changing structure of our economy also means that more help is necessary – by improving peoples' chances through education and training as well as simply meeting financial needs.

The policies we have looked at so far all have their costs as well as their benefits. Minimum wages may mean fewer jobs, higher taxes may reduce revenue and the benefit system combined with taxation causes the poverty trap.

One way of combining the merits of taxes and benefits is to run a scheme which integrates them. Social dividend, tax credits and negative income tax are all different ways of merging the two. The schemes work by everyone filling in a tax form and assessments are then made of the amount of tax that should be paid or the amount of benefit received. The advantage of this is that it removes means-tested benefits and the stigma associated with claiming the extra allowances available for the very poor. Provided that there is an overlap between tax and benefits, the effect of the poverty trap is reduced or removed as people do not lose all their benefit if they take a low-paid job. This provides more of an incentive to take a job even if the rewards are not great.

The same problem has arisen in all attempts to establish such schemes. If the level of benefit is to be adequate to raise all the poor above the poverty threshold, tax levels must rise substantially. This has generally met with political opposition. It seems difficult to devise a scheme which is simple to organise, redistributes income and reduces disincentives. Each alternative has implications for the trade-off between equity and efficiency.

There is no one solution to poverty. It requires a variety of techniques which cope with the different causes. Many of these policies just deal with the symptoms without really looking for a cure. A job with an adequate wage is the only real cure, but there will always be some people for whom this will be impossible, so government support will always be necessary.

9 Transport

Every Bank Holiday weekend the newspapers are full of tales of the misery inflicted upon those who want to 'get away from it all'. It seems that many have to content themselves with hours of much closer contact with others than they would have liked – in traffic queues on the motorways, in coaches and trains packed to capacity or in planes stacked high in the air while their pilots await a slot in the schedule. Being subjected to any of these delays is far from pleasant but the economic consequences of these transport inadequacies are more serious still.

The road and rail network in Britain has not kept pace with economic growth in the 1980s and the resulting congestion adds significantly to industry's costs. The South East generally and the Birmingham to Liverpool stretch of the M6 in particular have been most severely affected.

Transport has always faced the problem that it carries very little political weight. There are no votes in it because for every person you please there is someone who will never vote for you again. It takes ten years or more to carry out any plan and it costs a great deal of money.

An efficient transport network is an essential contributor to economic growth. It stimulates development by making places more accessible and facilitates it by helping to move goods more rapidly.

Decisions about the development of our transport network rely on economic evaluation of the various alternatives. Costs and benefits must be calculated. Changes in supply and demand all have external effects on people, industry and other forms of transport. This is clearly shown in the battle between road and rail transport in the UK, and for London in particular.

Roads

Any economy needs a road system that allows goods and people to be moved directly and with the minimum delay. In Britain, in recent years this has not happened. From 1977 to 1989 the demand for road space grew by 40 per cent but actual capacity has only increased by 5 per cent. The motorway network is almost a third longer, but traffic has risen by 108 per cent and we now have some of the most congested motorways in the developed world (Figure 9.1).

The planning system is designed to give everyone the opportunity to state their case but has often been used to delay major road building schemes. The M25 was originally planned to be the outer circle of three motorways, two of which were scrapped. It has taken more than twenty years for the road to be built so it is not surprising that it cannot cope with today's traffic.

FIGURE 9.1
The Growth of Motorway Traffic

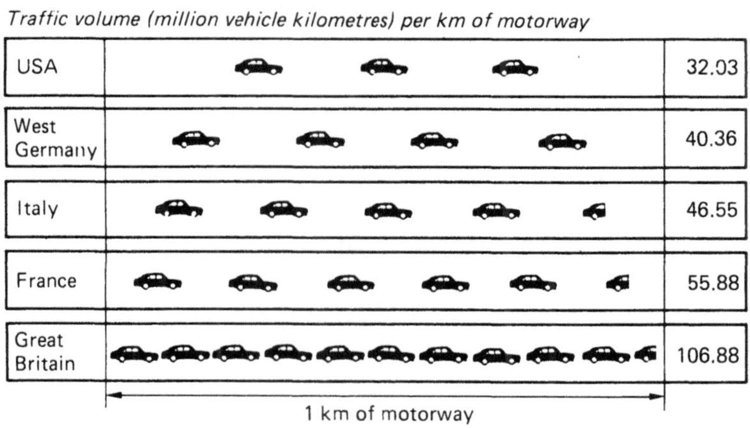

SOURCE: British Road Federation, *The Way Ahead* (n.d.).

Initial costs have always had to be kept to a minimum in order to be passed by the government department. This has often been a short-sighted plan because the whole-life costs have been much higher. In the long run, it is more expensive to build a two-lane motorway and have to add a third lane than building a three-lane motorway to start with. The extra cost of including the third lane is about £1.5m per mile but if it is added later it can cost up to £7m. It is now accepted that new roads create traffic, but this has not usually been taken into account so demand has been underestimated. Costs have also been kept down until recently by accepting a design-life of only twenty to thirty years. The first motorways were laid down in the 1960s, hence the constant roadworks which make our inadequate network even more congested.

More than one-third of the population of England and Wales now live in the South East. Fast economic growth has led to a disproportionate concentration of people and industry so most of the traffic jams are found there.

The costs of congestion are great. The Freight Transport Association has calculated the cost of jams on the M25. The road was designed for 85 000 vehicles a day and is carrying more than 130 000. The particularly congested section, south-west of London, has already had a fourth lane added. The FTA suggested, in 1988, that a lorry spends ninety hours a year in jams on this motorway, at a cost of £10 an hour. A total of 14 500 lorries a day pass through the most congested sections, which adds £13 million to industry's costs each year. It is not just a motorway problem. In Britain's conurbations, congestion is costing £3168 billion every year, according to the British Transport Federation.

These figures are arrived at by using data from the Department of Transport. Vehicle operating costs and working time are taken into account to produce Table 9.1.

The freight industry is the main source of complaint about the state of the road network. But freight traffic imposes a high cost in terms of wear and tear on the roads in return. One lorry does as much damage as around 250 000 cars.

The Way Forward?

The British Road Federation wants immediate action on a major

TABLE 9.1
Calculating the Cost of Congestion

	Resource Values (i.e. net of taxes) of Time per Vehicle *pence per hour (1986 prices)*
Working car	884.8
Non-working car	301.4
Average car	398.8
Light goods vehicle	618.9
Other goods vehicle	663.3
Public service vehicle	2994.3
Average vehicle	467.3

SOURCE: Department of Transport COBA 9, Assessments Policy and Methods Division.

road-building programme. The map in Figure 9.2 shows just how extensive this would be. It would result in great savings for industry as delivery times would be much reduced. The costs, however, would fall on other people's shoulders. The BRF would argue that if we want continued economic growth, these are the costs we would have to bear. Government has already agreed to meet the cost of some of these new roads in a £6 billion road-building scheme.

It takes about thirteen years for major road projects to be carried out and politicians tend to want immediate results. They will have to look further ahead if such new developments are to be approved.

The costs are not only financial but environmental as many hectares of land would disappear under concrete in the course of construction. Planning regulations would probably have to be relaxed if the schemes were to be carried out quickly enough to make any difference to the current problems. The environmental lobby would object strongly to such changes and would want the costs and benefits carefully weighed against each other. The road lobby and the environmentalists would hold very different sets of value judgements, so the planners would have to attempt to evaluate the different claims.

FIGURE 9.2
Future Road Development?

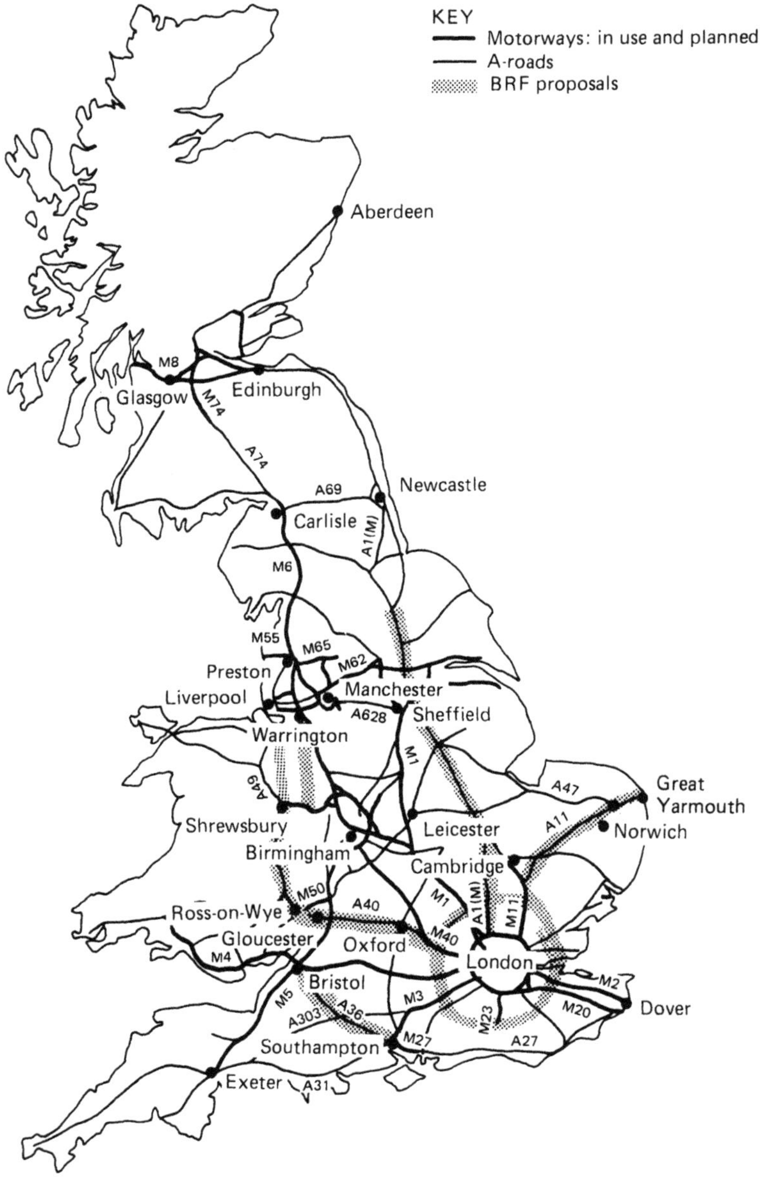

SOURCE: British Road Federation, *Building for Growth* (n.d.)

The problem is one of supply and demand. Demand is currently outstripping supply and there seems no prospect of equilibrium being reached without government intervention. Free market forces could reconcile this problem through price adjustments. Roads are provided by the state free to all users, however. No price is set, and so market pressures exist. Thus there are two alternatives: to increase supply or to reduce demand. Both these possibilities are being investigated.

Increasing supply

If more roads are to be built the money must be raised from either the private or the public sector. Many European countries have used private capital to finance motorway building, using tolls to recoup the outlay. This introduces market forces, at least, after a fashion. These ideas are starting to permeate the Department of Transport and the first experiments are under way. A private company is building a bridge across the Thames to take traffic away from the overloaded Dartford Tunnel.

There are suggestions for other ways in which the private sector might be involved but most seem problematical. Most companies would not be interested in being tied up for ten years or more in planning wrangles before their scheme could be carried out. The financial implications would be too great. A possibility would be for them to 'buy' a route when planning approval had been granted.

Ideas that are under consideration include a tunnel under the Thames from Chiswick to the East End and a second deck on the M25. The viability of the M25 plan has been called into question because it has been suggested that the tolls would have to be somewhere between £21 and £63 per motorist depending on the usage of the road.

If money is raised from the private sector, the Treasury may well take this into account and reduce the amount that the government provides. It may also prove to be more expensive because the government can borrow money more cheaply than the construction industry.

The road lobby constantly reminds the government that the taxes on road travel already contribute four times as much as is spent on road building, and asks why more of this cannot be used to improve the network.

Reducing demand

The rising trend in the demand for space on our roads is reflected in Figure 9.3.

Despite the fact that car ownership in Britain is running far behind the main industrialised countries of Europe and the USA, we still have some of the most congested roads. In 1988, there were 23 million cars in Britain so each one had an average of 56 feet of road! Various applications of the price mechanism are currently being considered. Charging for the use of motorways or for access to city centres would reduce demand. The alternative strategies that could be used will be investigated in the study of London's problems, later in the chapter.

FIGURE 9.3a
Who Owns a Car?

FIGURE 9.3b
Will There Be Room for All of Them?

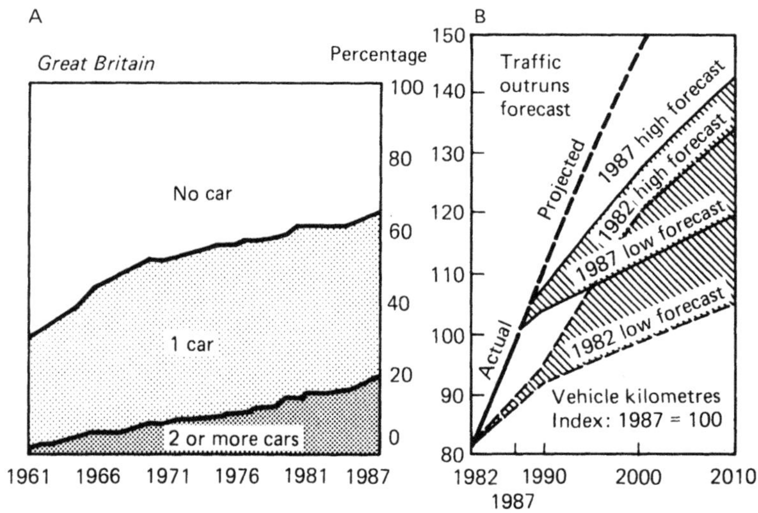

1 includes light vans

SOURCE: *Transport Statistics, Great Britain 1977–1987* (London: Department of Transport)

Instead of driving people away by high prices demand might be reduced by making the alternatives more attractive. The level of congestion seems to be related to the standard of public transport. If there is an efficient, integrated system people will leave their cars at home. The carrot could well be more effective than the stick of tolls and taxes.

The Railways

In the last thirty years, the railways have constantly lost out to road transport. The data in Figure 9.4a,b show the extent of their relative decline.

The actual change in rail usage has recently shown an upturn, but as a proportion of the total transport movements it is still falling. In other words, road transport is growing even faster.

FIGURE 9.4a
What's Happened to Rail Travel?

FIGURE 9.4b
Britain's Railways (% share of total transport movements)

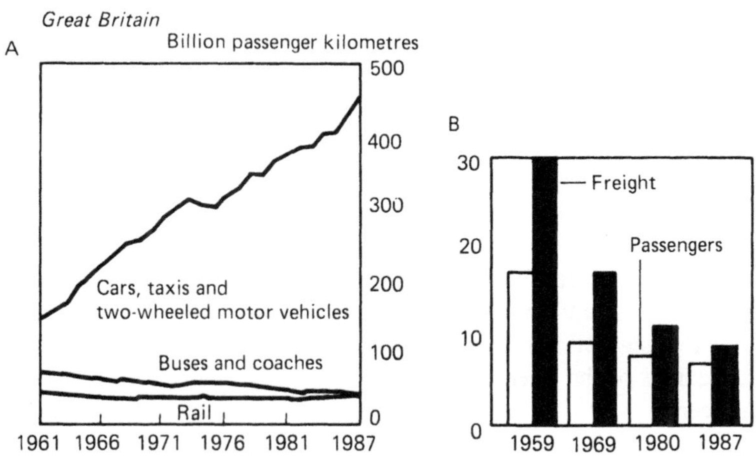

SOURCE: *Social Trends*, 1989; *Transport Statistics.*

Railways have always faced a debate about their role. Should they provide a social service or should they run on strictly economic lines, as they are now expected to do? The railway mania following the Industrial Revolution created an elaborate network of track. The profitability of the more remote routes was doubtful from the start. Once the railways were nationalised they were supported by government subsidies. The system has steadily been rationalised either by bankruptcy in the early days or by government decisions in more recent years.

Closures have always led to an outcry about the external effects on the locality as people without cars have relied on trains to get them to school, work or the shops. Many small seaside resorts used to depend on trains to bring in holiday-makers but lifestyles have changed and most people now have cars. As the railways have closed transport has become more difficult for those who do not drive.

If railways are to be regarded as a social service there has to be government funding. The current government firmly believes that the railways should pay their way and is steadily reducing the level of grant, in fact freight, parcels and the InterCity services have already lost their grants. There are some lines which can never be profitable but British Rail expects to go on running them on 'contract to the community', which really means financial assistance from national or local government. Efficiency will always be the key word.

The Future

Investment

Can railways help to reduce road congestion? The commuter services are faced with heavy loading at peak times of the day and the week. They have a market which finds alternative means of transport unacceptable. The pricing system as a result discriminates between these and more flexible passengers. Inelastic demand means that British Rail can charge higher prices in the rush hour and on some days of the week. The variation in price can be more than 100 per cent.

These high fares can be justified by looking at the marginal cost of providing the service. In order to maintain an adequate supply during the rush hour, British Rail needs to buy more trains and employ more people than it needs for the rest of the day. The cost of carrying each extra person is therefore high. In off-peak periods the train is probably half empty and the staff are employed for the shift anyway so the cost of carrying one extra passenger is low. Marginal cost pricing is an efficient policy because the price that the consumer pays is equal to the costs to society incurred in providing them with the service.

Despite the high fares there has been an upswing in demand which has led passengers to start complaining about overcrowding. There is no limit to how many tickets are sold for any train so rush hour journeys become increasingly unpleasant. The only way of overcoming this is to increase investment. A simple change, like making commuter trains longer, requires substantial investment because at many stations they are already as long as the platform. Figure 9.5 shows the level and direction of investment in British Rail into the early 1990s. £3.8 billion sounds as if there will be great improvements but when compared with Germany, where investment stands at £4.5 billion in twelve months and the USA, where almost £2 billion is being spent on one line from Boston to Washington, changes do not seem so significant.

The Channel Tunnel rail link may persuade freight traffic to move to the railways because the proposed high-speed European rail network will connect Britain with the whole of Europe. Before this can happen, rail links round London will have to be improved. It is anticipated that the main benefits would arise in peak times but would, of course, not lead to a truck free Kent!

Privatisation

The railways have long been thought of as a natural monopoly because of the economies of scale inherent in the system. The size of the network should mean that the costs of supplying the service could be lower than if it were run in smaller units which would have to duplicate some of the investment. But by the mid-1990s the government expects to have sold British Rail thus leaving the market to cope with the problems of lack of capacity. It may move from being a public monopoly to a private one if it sold off as one unit. Alternatively, it could revert to the regional companies from which it originated. A third possibility is to create a track authority which would hire out track space to companies which ran the trains.

FIGURE 9.5a
British Rail Investment

FIGURE 9.5b
Where Is the Money Going?

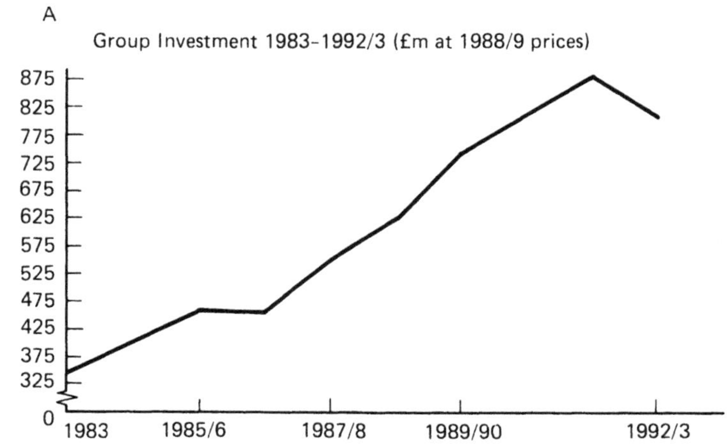

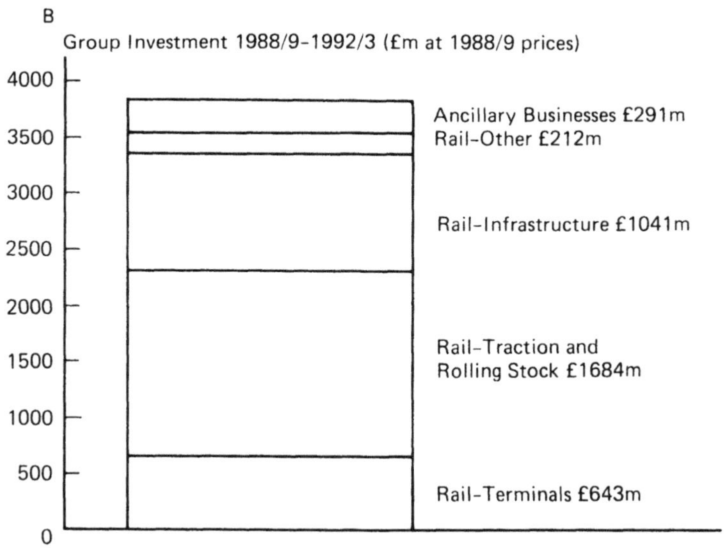

SOURCE: *British Rail Corporate Plan*, British Rail Publications, London, July 1988.

Protagonists of privatisation suggest that it will bring in more investment because a more efficient service will lead to greater returns, but the routes which will never make a profit will be under threat or will have to be subsidised by the government.

Road v. Rail: The Costs

Roads and railways have to meet very different criteria when investment schemes are assessed for viability.

When a new road is planned it is valued on a cost–benefit basis. The benefits of reduced journey time, less congestion and less pollution are all taken into account. Figure 9.6 comes from the Department of Transport and only includes construction costs but gives an idea of the balance of costs and benefits. It is much more difficult for a railway development to prove itself viable because only the costs and revenues are calculated and in the 1980s an 8 per cent return had to be achieved on the investment. Whether the new line will make life better for people in terms of their environment, speed or costs is given some consideration because 8 per cent is less than a commercial return on investment, but unlike roads a return is still expected.

As competition between them is inequitable it means that roads are built more readily because they appear to be relatively cheaper. This differential creates even more inequality because as the subsidy to British Rail is removed, the passengers have to bear the full cost. Road users, however, do not. All they pay are the private costs, i.e. the costs of their time and of running their car (Figure 9.7). The more congested a road becomes, the higher the social costs, because each car contributes to delay and pollution but these are ignored.

If each road user paid the real or marginal social costs of driving a car, the price would rise considerably and therefore demand might fall. Travelling by train would then become more attractive as it would seem relatively less expensive and demand would probably rise.

As things stand at the moment, resources are not being allocated efficiently because of the distortion of prices. More people use the roads because they appear cheap; fewer people use the railway because it seems expensive, so resources have been used to build roads and not railways.

FIGURE 9.6
Costs and Benefits of Road Construction

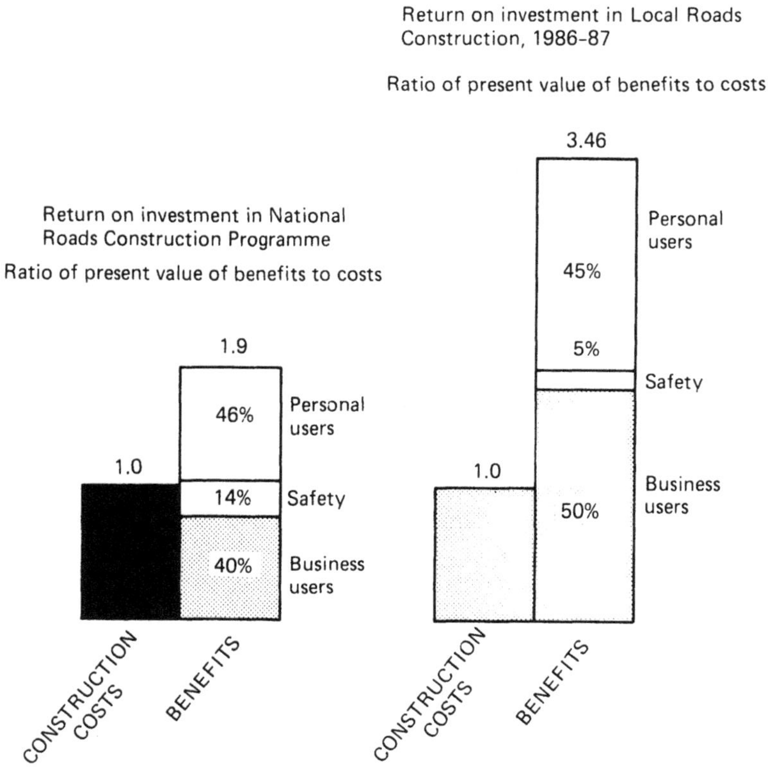

SOURCE: British Road Federation, *The Cost of Congestion* (n.d.).

Competition or Integration?

If transport is left entirely to market forces, more and more people will drive cars because at present their ownership disregards externalities. The individual driver will look at the private costs and ignore the effects on the environment. Car tax, petrol tax and the annual road fund licence are a contribution but do not cover the costs incurred by motorists. Social costs are, therefore, much higher than

FIGURE 9.7
The Private and Social Costs of Car Ownership

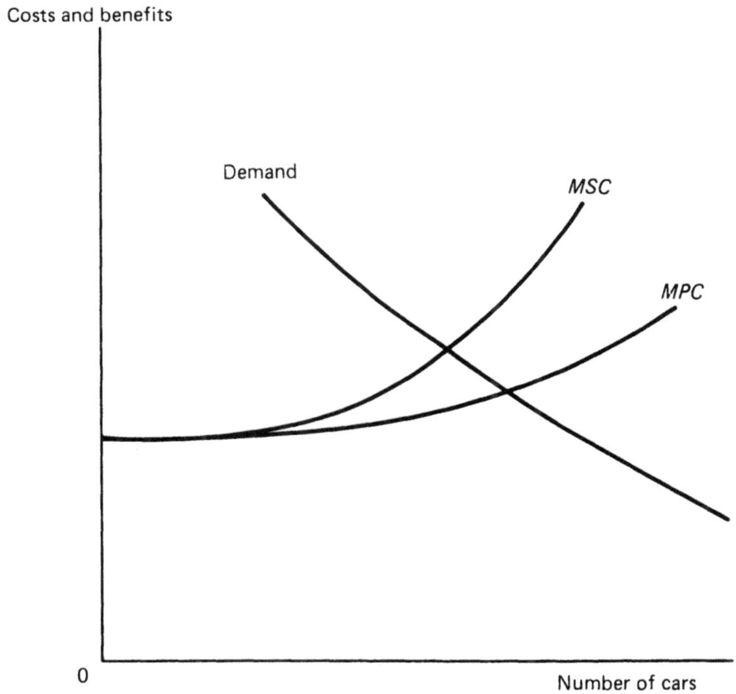

private costs. As more people own cars the government will feel the need to build more roads.

A comparison of marginal social costs and benefits of more roads or more railways would probably lead to a different allocation of resources as the negative externalities of more roads and cars are considerable.

People need cars when public transport is inadequate, so an efficient integrated system could reduce the problems of congested roads. Can the solutions, already discussed, really work in a city where the congestion described in the next article is commonplace?

FRUSTRATIONS AT HIGH NOON ON A CLOGGED-UP CLEARWAY

It is close to noon on Chiswick High Road, west London, one of Britain's most congested thoroughfares. Its status as an urban clearway is a motorist's and traffic engineer's joke.

Metropolitan Police Constables 216 and 218 are on station, with the job of keeping traffic moving from Hammersmith through to the junction of the North Circular Road, A4 and M4 at Gunnersbury roundabout by Kew Bridge.

A taxi pulls up to collect a passenger and blocks one of the two lanes into London. A motorist stops to chat to the taxi driver, blocking the other lane. A jam develops and from it a woman in a Granada Ghia pulls over to the wrong side of the road to seek directions from the officers – blocking a 237 bus on its way to Shepherds Bush.

Having been advised and admonished, she mounts the pavement to avoid the bus and carves her way back into her proper lane. As she does so a van parks on a yellow line between a zebra crossing and a bus stop.

The police say the traffic flow has improved since they began towing away between thirty and forty cars a day. Bus drivers welcomed the move; shop keepers say trade has been affected.

The situation on Chiswick High Road is a daily lesson on how the capital, and by extension Britain, effectively has no policy for urban roads.

Chiswick's main thoroughfare has become a road to appall the theorists who a generation ago urged the separation of through and local traffic and of pedestrians and vehicles. The High Road is a muddle of all: an artery into the capital, a shopping street, a bus route and a dispersal point for people, prams, wheelchairs and drivers off the M4 who have lost their way.

Adapted from *The Times*, 10 October, 1988.

The Problem

1.25m commuters enter London every day

Demand for rail travel up by 15%

Demand for underground travel up by 42%

162 000 people commute in cars

2.1m vehicles cross London's outer boundary

1.5m vehicles enter London's central area

Source *Transport Statistics for London* (HMSO, 1989).

London's traffic moves at an average speed of 11 mph. Economic growth in the 1980s has caused increasing problems for London's traffic. It travels no faster now than in the days of hansom cabs. Transportation has suffered from being the poor relation in planning. It has always been a difficult issue because of the constraints of existing roads and buildings but without an effective transport network the city cannot flourish.

We are again faced with a demand and supply problem to which there are three alternative solutions:

1. Reduce demand;
2. Increase supply;
3. Make better use of the resources we have.

How can demand be reduced?

Currently, the number of people who commute to London by car is falling. Demand is being rationed by congestion. As the time taken rises, more people take the train. This is an inefficient method of controlling demand because the economic and social side-effects of congestion are legion. A figure of £1451 million has been estimated as the cost of congestion in London but this takes no account of externalities such as noise, pollution and road accidents. Police attribute the growing amount of reckless driving to frustration caused by traffic jams. There are 500 deaths, 5000 serious injuries and 50 000 less serious injuries every year, so the social costs involved are very high.

Charging drivers for the use of roads is one way of controlling congestion. A price for driving into congested areas at peak times would deter the marginal user as it would make them consider the external costs as well as the private costs of their actions. The drawback of rationing by price is that it leads to inequality of access as the less well-off would have to leave their cars at home. It could be justified if transport were treated as one market because the revenue from charging motorists could then be used to improve the whole system and therefore benefit everyone, thus improving efficiency overall.

Finding a system of tolls which works efficiently has proved difficult. Many cities around the world have tried limiting the number of cars but the results are not always straightforward. In Singapore, a full car does not pay a toll to enter the city so street urchins now have a steady income from hiring themselves out as passengers. Cars with odd and even registration numbers are allowed into Lagos on alternate days, so the rich have two cars and the corrupt have two number plates.

One alternative is to insert sensors in the road and an 'electronic number plate' to each car. Every time the car passes the sensor its number is registered and a bill is sent each month. There are substantial costs involved in setting up and running such a scheme and it is rather inflexible.

Charging for access to city centres is politically problematical because people do not like paying for something they are used to getting for nothing. Things would have to get a lot worse in London before road pricing became acceptable.

Reducing demand on the railways by raising prices would drive more people on to the roads, or if it were done in conjunction with road pricing it would destroy the commercial and social life of the capital.

Can supply increase?

By the year 2001 forecasts suggest that car traffic in London will rise by 10 per cent and demand for rail and underground journeys is likely to increase by 15 to 20 per cent.

There is little scope for additional road building in central London unless swathes of buildings are knocked down or some of our precious open spaces disappear beneath concrete. Proposals to build roads through areas like Islington and Barnes meet with very vociferous and effective pressure groups composed of television personalities, senior civil servants and city folk. They know how to get their own way.

Expansion of the railway network is a more promising route. There are plans to spend more than £3 billion on the rail and underground network. The money will mainly have to come from fares and the private sector but the government has shown a change of direction in its attitude to railway funding. They will provide money if there are non-user benefits such as relief of road congestion.

How can current resources be used more effectively?

Any transport network is an interdependent system. Alterations to one sector will affect the functioning of the others. A new road will lead to a reduction in rail users, while cheaper fares on the trains mean that people leave their cars at home.

In order to persuade people to travel by train rather than road, the journey has to be made as easy, cheap and comfortable as possible. Both rail and underground are being refurbished and attempts made to speed up access. The introduction of tickets which allow travellers to use all modes of transport in London gives people flexibility and prevents them standing in queues at each interchange. They have also increased demand because the marginal cost to the individual of an extra journey has fallen to zero. A travel card allows the holder to travel within certain zones, not just a fixed journey to work, so people make more use of it at no extra cost. The marginal cost, to the railway system, of the extra usage is also zero because it is generally at off-peak times.

The system must become more integrated so that passengers can transfer directly from one mode of transport to another. To be really effective this needs more investment. Relatively small amounts have so far enabled rail travellers to cross London directly, for example via the Thameslink line, instead of having to transfer between trains by taxi or underground.

A combination of increasing the supply and efficiency of the whole of London's transport network will help to overcome both current congestion and future growth in demand. Pricing roads will be used as a last resort if the other solutions fail to work. It would be more effective to tempt people away from their cars by the provision of a better alternative than creating a system which people tried to evade.

The government is not in favour of central planning for transport because it is believed that once plans are made they are inflexible and do not adapt to changing circumstances. There is, however, a strong argument for more integration of the systems especially if new investment is to be used efficiently.

London has, as yet, been excluded from bus deregulation but the system has been influenced considerably by the pressures for change which have arisen in neighbouring areas. Hereford was originally selected for an experiment in deregulation in an attempt to introduce competition to the bus services. The scheme was later introduced to the rest of the country.

The next section investigates deregulation and attempts to evaluate its successes and failures in increasing efficiency.

A Free Market for Buses?

The aim of bus deregulation was to reduce the level of monopoly power, increase competition and cut government spending. Under the previous system, a well-established operator was protected from competition because both price and quantity could be controlled and other firms could not enter the market. The Traffic Commissioners controlled the supply of Road Service Licences (RSV) and this gave them a say in both fare levels and schedules. Firms holding an RSV had protection from competition as long as they kept the rules.

The demand for bus services had declined steadily as the number of cars rose. In the ten years before deregulation the subsidy rose by 238 per cent to £897 million. The government was keen to reduce this burden by introducing more competition.

By 1985, RSVs had been abolished for both long-distance coaches and local buses, apart from in London. Firms had to register the route and timing of their service, the National Bus Company was privatised and municipal buses had to be run as separate companies. Unprofitable services had to be tendered for and the firm with the lowest tender would be paid to run the route.

Has Monopoly Power Been Removed?

Monopoly exists when there is only one supplier. Barriers to entry allow it to continue. A bus company which had won a contract to provide buses for a particular route was in this position. A monopolist can decide either how much to produce or the selling price of the product. If the aim is to maximise profit, a lower output will mean that people will be prepared to pay a higher price, especially when demand is inelastic. If output is restricted, the firm will not be using its factors of production efficiently so resources will be misallocated.

The legal barriers to entry have been abolished so any firm that meets the requirements and has calculated that it will make a profit can register a route. There is competition for the unprofitable routes as the subsidy will go to the firm with the lowest tender.

The initial reaction to deregulation in Glasgow was too much competition and the streets were blocked with buses. This gradually sorted itself out and the trend in many areas seems to be towards concentration. There is also evidence of other practices which aim to reduce the effects of competition. Some companies have become very acquisitive. Front Source of Aldershot and Stagecoach in Perth have been involved in take-overs and the central topic of conversation in the industry has been of mergers.

There have also been complaints about predatory pricing. Larger firms run a route at a loss in order to drive out the competition from smaller firms and then regain their monopoly power. Some companies have introduced travel cards and multiride tickets so their passengers are tied to them. This can only be done if one company runs a substantial network of buses.

Competition may also be thwarted by collusion. If the market is dominated by a few large firms they may try to share out routes and fix prices. This suggests that the industry is really an oligopoly. If the tendency towards oligopoly continues, the Office of Fair Trading will have to step in to control practices which reduce competition. They have already been involved in the issue of predatory pricing.

What has happened to prices?

Removing monopoly power suggests that abnormal profits should disappear and prices should fall. This did not happen. On average they rose by 9 per cent in the year after deregulation and in South Yorkshire by 238 per cent. This was not altogether the effect of deregulation. It coincided with rate capping so councils could no longer subsidise buses to the extent that they had in the past, therefore fares rose. Price cutting was more evident in the long-distance coach services.

Output has to be measured in two ways. Figure 9.8 shows that the number of vehicle miles has risen throughout the country. The use of minibuses has greatly increased and there are now routes to places

FIGURE 9.8
What Has Happened to Output?

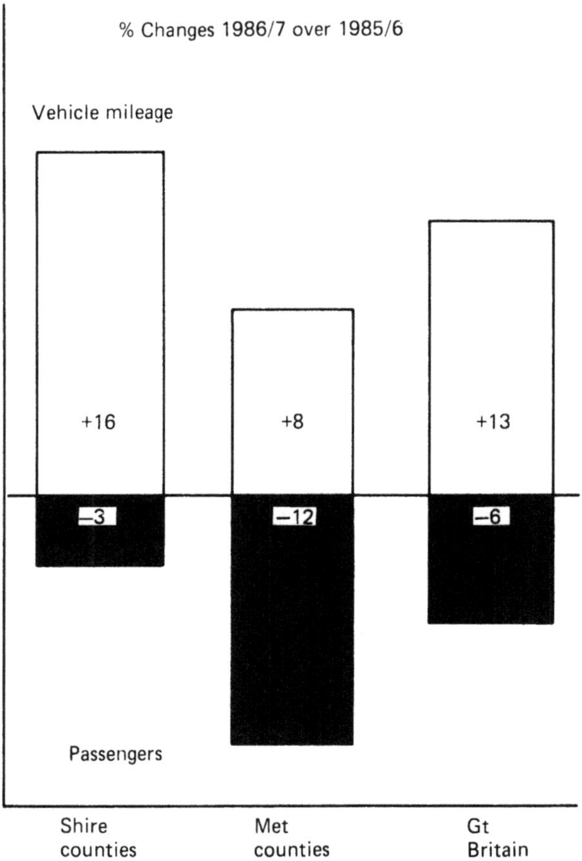

SOURCE: Transport and Road Research Laboratory.

which standard buses could never reach. This is definitely an improvement as more people have closer access to a service.

Some of this rise can be accounted for by schedule matching when two companies run buses at the same time so that they each have a share of trade at peak periods. However, this does not improve the service overall as for most of the day things have not changed.

The figures do not show the loss of weekend services and the effect of the change on the integrated network. Although buses were famed for running in threes and being erratic, the system was planned as a whole and services interconnected. Now that individual companies run the routes integration has largely disappeared and passengers complain that they don't know when buses are supposed to run. Timetables seem few and far between.

The second way of evaluating output is by usage. The number of passengers has fallen substantially since deregulation. Price has been the main factor. Earlier in the chapter we noted that more people now travel by train. Rising bus fares and the slow pace of city traffic have both encouraged this trend.

It seems likely that as the system settles down and the initial increase in prices levels out people will return to the buses, especially if they are running on more convenient routes.

Has efficiency improved?

The threat of competition should lead firms to look at their costs. A monopolist does not have to worry too much about costs especially when local authorities are committed to low bus fares and therefore subsidise the service.

The introduction of minibuses can reduce costs by half as they are cheaper to buy and run, and their drivers are paid less than those on full-size buses.

Labour costs have been reduced by cutting holiday and sickness pay as well as reducing the workforce. The latter has become possible through flexible rostering by which staff work in shifts which fit more closely with the demand for buses.

Companies have also become more aware of the maintenance time for buses. The opportunity cost of a full-sized bus being off the road for a week is very high. They cost almost £100 000 each and if they earn no revenue for a week the company's profits are hit. There was a suspicion that this would lead to lower standards but as yet there is no evidence to prove this. There are now more vehicle examiners and the number of spot checks has risen.

What has happened to subsidies?

The government aimed to reduce the level of subsidies and it has succeeded. In the first year after deregulation they fell by £40 million and have fallen further subsequently.

Under the regulated system, companies were expected to use some of their monopoly profit to subsidise routes which were not economically viable but were felt to be socially necessary. They were also expected to charge the same rate per mile for all services, however much they were used. Now that these firms have lost their monopoly power and become more efficient, this no longer happens. The National Bus Company suggested that £122 million might be lost in cross-subsidisation of its routes. From the economists point of view, this has been saved as the system no longer produces the monopoly profits which allow it to happen.

Until the new system has been running for several years it will be impossible to give a full evaluation but it seems, at the moment, to be succeeding in the provision of services, reducing both costs and subsidies. The costs of improvements may be passed on to the consumer when the initial effect of rate capping has faded and passengers return to the buses.

Deregulation has failed to provide the level of competition that was hoped for as firms seem to have a natural tendency to create imperfections in the market, in order to protect themselves and maintain an element of monopoly power.

On the Right Tracks?

Transport must be looked at as a whole because the different modes are inevitably interrelated. Buses, trains and cars are direct substitutes. If the price of one rises, demand for the others will rise and vice versa. This degree of change will vary according to the elasticity of demand.

In some parts of the country bus fares have been heavily subsidised resulting in a rise in demand. Were people making more journeys or changing from other forms of transport? The answer is a combination of the two. If cheap and efficient public transport can persuade people to leave their cars at home, congestion can be reduced. But these cheap fares have to be paid for and it is the local taxpayer who bears the brunt. In London, the system was criticised because many of the people who benefited were commuters who did not pay London taxes. Londoners complained that this was inequitable. However, there may be positive externalities in providing cheap public transport – we will not need more roads, car parks, traffic police, etc. For some people and goods, road transport is unavoidable and reduced congestion will make their journeys faster and therefore cheaper.

Privatisation and deregulation are alternative solutions and are regarded as techniques of making the system more efficient. The removal of restrictions from long-distance coach travel has increased competition and reduced prices but the effect on local services has been more mixed. The results of railway privatisation will not be apparent until the late 1990s, if then.

10 Success or Failure?

Have social policy and the economic tools that are used to analyse it really worked? In this final chapter we will evaluate these two themes.

Does Economic Theory Really Help Decision-making?

The calculation of costs and benefits is the main technique used when deciding to carry out a new scheme. Methods have become steadily more sophisticated as time has passed but there are still problems associated with it.

What should be included?

Every new scheme has effects both direct and indirect. Deciding which ones to include in the calculations is a difficult task because everyone will put a different ranking on them. The researchers have to make a decision based on the cost of the work and their assessment of each effect.

How do we measure value?

In order to make the calculations more tangible a money value is given to each effect that is to be included. In order to do this, an estimate is made of the compensation that people would accept for the change in their way of life. In other words, they are trying to put a market value on each cost. The problem arises when people say, 'No money on earth will make up for the new railway line running through my house.' It is easy enough to put a value on the house but the disruption is more difficult to cope with.

Benefits to society cause an even greater problem because they are even more intangible. Consumer surplus has been used extensively in cost–benefit analysis in order to overcome this. If people are prepared to pay more than the asking price for a particular commodity then they are gaining. This gain is known as the consumer surplus. The shaded area in Figure 10.1 shows this gain.

FIGURE 10.1
Consumer Surplus

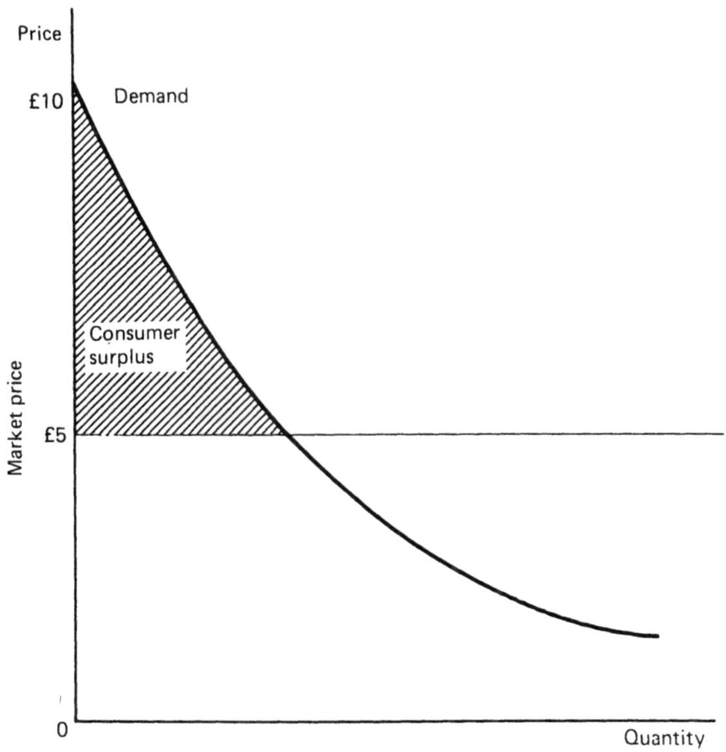

The techniques that they use are by no means perfect but are better than none.

Who reaps the benefit, who pays the costs?

If the same group of people paid the costs and received the benefits, it would be easier to decide whether a project was viable. When these groups are different the problem is more complicated. How do we compare the benefit of the businessmen who travel to Brussels more quickly with the loss of a village community?

When do we count the costs and benefits?

The Channel Tunnel is expected to be ready in 1993, but the benefits from it will be spread over an indefinite length of time. How should we attempt to count them? Because most people would prefer to receive the benefits immediately, the further away they are, the lower their value. Investors would have to be paid more in the future to compensate for this. This is known as discounting and it is not a straightforward process. Different costs and benefits may need different discount rates. The rate chosen may affect the viability of the project. If future benefits are regarded as low, the project is less likely to be acceptable; if they are high, it is more likely to go ahead. As money changes value over time an estimate of inflation must also be incorporated into the calculations.

Many of the problems mentioned above crop up in other methods of evaluating spending. When using input–output analysis in education, a value has to be given to the different forms of output. As no way has been found of measuring abstract achievement, exam results have proved to be the basis for calculation. Although this is the way the outside world tends to access schools, their aims are usually much broader.

The use of QALYs is perhaps more successful because they put a value on the quality of life that a particular procedure will give. Even this can only be a rough yardstick because everyone is different. Accident victims with similar injuries may recover at very different rates, some may make miraculous recoveries while others are handicapped for life.

What must be considered when using scarce resources is that it is better to use some systematic form of allocation rather than allowing it to be random. Everyone must, however, realise the limitations of the process and not be rigidly ruled by it when it is seen to fail. Economic theory is useful when used with caution. It cannot hope to cater for individual differences but provides an excellent guideline for broader issues.

Social Policy: Enterprise Culture v. Nanny State?

TABLE 10.1
The Most Important Things In Life

	First	*Second*	*Third*	*Fourth*	*Fifth*
Finland	Health	Love	Peace of mind	Happy family	Job security
France	Health	Success	Happy family	Love	Friends
Germany	Health	Friends	Happy family	Love	Free time
Italy	Health	Happy family	Job	Success	Money
Spain	Health	Happy family	Love	Friends	Success/ money
Sweden	Health	Love	Friends	Happy family	Fun
UK	Health	Happy family	Money	Friends	Success

SOURCE: McCann Erickson, *The New Generation* (Worldwide, 1989).

Young people all over Europe were asked to list the five most important things in life (Table 10.1). The British ranked money higher than anyone else; in fact five other countries didn't include it in their top five at all. Ten years ago no one rated it highly. Why do

Swedes and Germans ignore the materialistic features of life? Why do attitudes vary so much?

Can the Market Work?

There is always a degree of self-interest in people's behaviour. Instinct tells us that self-preservation is important so in many circumstances decision-making is far from altruistic. In times of economic stringency people seem more inclined to 'look after number one'.

Most of the 1980s have been characterised as the era of enterprise. People have apparently become more selfish and materialistic. These are perhaps the attitudes which make the economy grow. In a competitive market the owners of businesses will try to make them run efficiently to achieve maximum profits. They are unlikely to produce at allocative or productive efficiency because the market will not be perfect. However, they will be interested in keeping their costs as low as possible for fear of competition. As firms get bigger, costs can be reduced even further by increasing economies of scale. These trends benefit the owners of the firms and may be passed on to the customers in the form of lower prices or better quality. The side-effect of this is a changing distribution of income. As the market is allowed free rein, people who work in the growing sectors of the economy gain while the rest are lucky to hold their own. The north–south divide is evidence of this changing pattern. In the public sector, wages are not determined by the market so they tend to get left behind. Growth may also be at the expense of the environment if the market is left to itself because goods can be produced more cheaply if these problems are ignored.

In the late 1980s, most people became more affluent and there is some evidence of changing attitudes. More has been given to charity through Band Aid and Comic Relief than ever before. Growing awareness of the damage we are doing to our environment is beginning to influence our habits. Table 10.2 shows evidence of these changes. Do we become more caring as we grow more affluent?

By spending more to buy products which do less damage, negative externalities are turned into private costs. If markets always worked like that, there would be a chance of achieving efficiency.

In a perfect world, demand would equal marginal social benefit

TABLE 10.2
Environmental Issues: Consumers Changing Attitudes

Would you be prepared to:	
Pay an extra 2p per gallon of petrol to help reduce air pollution?	1987 41% 1989 52%
Have an increase in income tax of 1p in the pound to pay for measures to protect the environment and conserve natural resources?	1987 34% 1989 49%
Pay an extra £5 per year on your electricity bill to help reduce acid rain?	1987 18% 1989 37%
Stop buying wood products made from trees such as teak and mahogany unless it could be guaranteed that they came from countries that were protecting their forests?	1987 25% 1989 35%

SOURCE: MORI-COLMAN-RSCG.

and supply would equal marginal social cost. If this happened, we would have both economic and social efficiency. *But the world is not perfect!* As we have seen throughout the book, markets fail because the conditions for perfection are impossible to achieve.

People do not have perfect knowledge and therefore what they buy does not give the greatest benefit. They are often influenced by advertising in a way that is hard to describe as rational. The paternalistic view would be that there is a mismatch between what people want and what they need.

The fact that there are externalities means that demand and marginal social benefits will be different. In the cases of health and education, the benefits would be greater than demand because their influence spreads further than the individual consumer. This is reversed for demerit goods such as alcohol and tobacco.

The supply side also suffers imperfections. Monopoly and oligopoly mean that new firms cannot enter the market because of the costs of advertising, the sheer size of the capital investment needed to start production and many other factors. In addition, the labour market is guilty of imperfections, as we have seen in the explanation of income distribution. All these factors keep prices apart from the levels needed for economic efficiency and therefore misallocate resources.

Every firm which adds to pollution and every car which adds to congestion contributes to the difference between supply and marginal social cost. These externalities mean that all the costs are not being covered and people want to buy more than if they were paying the full price. Again resources are misallocated and the system is inefficient.

Each chapter has shown how difficult it is for the market alone to achieve efficiency. Equity is even harder to accomplish. Because each individual starts with different attributes, a market system is most unlikely to make things fairer.

Freedom of choice is often claimed as a key objective of the free market system, but it often fails to meet this criterion. If resources are limited, they are simply rationed by price and this gives freedom of choice to those who can afford them.

Can the Government Do Better?

There can be no automatic assumption that government intervention will improve things. The state usually aims to improve equity when it interferes with the market mechanism. In almost every chapter we have seen such policies. The problem is that there are winners and losers every time.

When rents are controlled, to protect tenants, they are pushed below the equilibrium level and supply is cut. The winners are those who already have a house or flat. They benefit from cheaper housing. The losers suffer because landlords stop letting and sell up, so they have no home at any price.

When minimum wage levels are established, if demand is elastic, there will be fewer jobs. The winners are those who keep their jobs because their wages are higher. The losers are those who no longer have a job.

If these situations arise there may be no overall gain in equity and if the government takes no further action the losers face considerably more problems. Controls must therefore be used as part of a package to increase employment or provide more housing in order to mitigate the side-effects.

Taxes and subsidies are an alternative means of control but these have their problems. If demand is inelastic and supply elastic, a tax puts up the price almost as much, so the affluent can continue to buy whereas limitations are imposed on the poor. If traffic must be controlled in city centres, an entry fee might be thought appropriate. This would certainly reduce traffic by cutting out those who could not afford it. Again the aims of the government may be achieved but at the expense of equity.

Thus we have a system which is neither equitable nor efficient.

Which Works Better?

Both 'Enterprise Culture' and 'Nanny State' are used as terms of abuse by those who oppose them. The Enterprise Culture smacks of an uncaring, money-grubbing society where people no longer matter and all is sacrificed for the sake of profit. The Nanny State, on the other hand, wraps people in cotton wool so that they have no decisions to make for themselves and therefore stifles initiative and efficiency. There is some truth in both sides of the argument and as policies become more extreme the results bear more resemblance to these caricatures. In order to evaluate the two options the question must be asked, 'Do they meet their objectives?'

The enterprise economy would claim to make things better for everyone in the long run because the country would be efficient and industry would thrive. Free markets would mean that industry would move to the poorer areas because land and labour would be cheap. People would leave industries with low wages so a falling labour supply would push pay up. Equilibrium would be achieved and everyone would benefit.

We have seen many times over that efficiency cannot be achieved because markets fail and the effort to attain it can be expensive on equity.

A government which takes a much more positive role in all sectors of the economy would be aiming at a more equitable way of life. There would be more intervention in areas where there are current disparities. All the issues we have looked at would be subject to more controls and manipulation in order to achieve greater equity.

In some areas equity might well improve. A more progressive tax structure would be fairer but would the trade-off be less efficiency, smaller incomes and a smaller tax revenue? Some attempts at increased equity succeed for some but make things worse for others.

This debate brings us back to the issue of value judgements because they will determine the relative importance that the individual places on different alternatives.

In Britain, we are unlikely to move away from a market economy but the degree of intervention will be determined by the value judgements of the population. The market mechanism has the great advantage that it works cheaply and efficiently, but its failure needs to be tempered by government intervention in order to reduce the social problems that face people who slip through the net.

The following quotation from Charles Schultze sums up the problem of deciding which is best: 'In all cases the comparison should be between an imperfect market and an imperfect government, not some ideal abstraction.'

Index

www.ingramcontent.com/pod-product-compliance
Ingram Content Group UK Ltd.
Pitfield, Milton Keynes, MK11 3LW, UK
UKHW020837290926
15470UKWH00004B/1398